book *idea* to
BESTSELLER
in 30 Days

MICHAEL D. BUTLER

You want to be a best-selling author, right? Just the name sounds great, doesn't it? Of course, being able to call yourself a best-selling author and put that on your Facebook bio, business card, or LinkedIn profile is certain to impress colleagues, friends, and family. For many, it's much more than that; it's not just having the title of best-selling author. It's about being able to charge more for coaching, consulting, and speaking, as well as being able to get more speaking gigs, more radio and TV interviews, and being seen as an expert in their field.

A best-selling book's ability to establish your credibility is invaluable, and, in the post-Borders Bookstore age, there are more best-selling authors than ever. You could be next!

What others are saying about....
BOOK IDEA TO BESTSELLER

"I just wanted to be an author. I had no idea I could go best-seller, but it feels great and has opened up so many doors."

Melodieann Whiteley

"Michael and his team dramatically help authors increase book sales and is one of the top leaders of this industry."

Brian Tracy, Business Expert

"I'm referring authors to you, because I know you will take good care of them."

Jim Stovall, Founder of the Emmy-Award Winning Narrative Television Network, 20 million books sold, and named "one of the most outstanding men of our era" by Steve Forbes

"Getting a movie deal was more than I could have ever dreamed! Thank you!"

Pamala Kennedy, More Than Rice-Human Trafficking

"THANK YOU all from the bottom of my heart for helping "Dorm Room To Millionaire" hit #1 BEST SELLER in business and in money categories!"

Alex Morton, Dorm Room to Millionaire

"I wish I had known about you two years ago! Our numbers are way up!"

Dr. Eve Agee

"Our numbers are up – yeah!"

Arielle Ford, Author, Speaker, Publicist

"It was a pleasure working with you and your team. Thanks for getting my book to #1."

Dave Ferguson, author of Boss or Leader

"There are many self-proclaimed gurus out there, but Michael is the real deal!"

Glenn Sparks, former Dallas Cowboy

"I can't say enough about Beyond Publishing and what they did for me to get my book, Pineville Heist, as a #1 best-selling thriller on Amazon. I have had 40,000 downloads and gained 60,000 Twitter followers, and I owe almost all of that to Michael D. Butler's team at Beyond Publishing,
Check them out!"

Lee Chambers, Canadian Film Director and Author
The Pineville Heist

TABLE OF CONTENTS

INTRODUCTION

The journey into the publishing world happened for me in 2018 when I published my first book **The Single Dad's Survival Guide**. I had already written **Bestseller Status – Becoming a Bestselling Author in the Digital Age** and that book has helped thousands write their book, get bestseller status not to mention global distribution. Father's Day was coming up and I decided to release **Single Dad's Survival Guide** first and that turned out to be a good choice but releasing **Bestseller Status** would soon confirm that starting a publishing company was the right decision for me. That was just 6 years ago, and we have gone on to publish 791 titles by authors in 64 nations and our authors have spoken on six continents.

As our publishing company and readership grew, we started getting inquiries from around the world from authors who wanted to know how to write a bestseller, how to market a bestseller and how to get global distribution. We began recording those questions and noticed a pattern, most of the questions fell into one of three categories. Authors wanted to know how to write a bestseller, how to market a bestseller and how to get global distribution.

I included much of the data from that early feedback in **Bestseller Status – Becoming a Bestselling Author in the Digital Age** and include some of it here to bring the reader up to speed with how the internet has transformed readership and global book publishing. From here I went on to feature a video series on YouTube called www.**52AuthorSecrets.com** formerly 52AuthorTips.com addressing each one of these questions in a one-minute video. Those videos are the basis of the book you now hold in your hands.

Many people thought the internet killed publishing, the truth is readership is up globally and knowledge is doubling monthly in many industries. The best way to create credibility with a topic is to publish a book on that topic. Writing and publishing a book on a subject can make you the expert in that space. But there's more than that, you can create an entire business and movement around each book you write.

You will see me use the titles **Book Idea to Bestseller in 30 Days** and **Bestseller Status** interchangeably because they are one and the same. Depending on what you need in the moment. Grab a hold of all the great content I've created on this topic, follow our videos online at www.**52AuthorSecrets. com** and keep learning. We'll keep adding to this content and aggregating it for you as things change in the market and new tools are available for you. You'll notice some of these Secrets

I say what country or beach I'm on, this is because literally for me as an author and book publisher business never stops when I'm traveling in fact, that's the reason I am traveling, because travel ignites my inner creative! Not to mention since we have authors in 59 nations and growing. Many weeks we are flying somewhere around the world to support our authors with their book launches or attending a major book show in some exotic cities like in Israel, Italy, Mexico, Colombia, Germany, Poland or any other exciting place you can think of.

When you watch the videos I did with each of these secrets at www.**52AuthorSecrets.com** you'll be able to see exactly where I was shooting all around the world from: Dubai, London, Greece, Costa Rica, Jerusalem and many more. And if you're the overachiever and want to skip the line you can jump right into my course that I created during the pandemic to help hundreds, now thousands write their bestselling book in just one hour at **www.CredibilityBook.Live**

Why I'm a Writer Today

Growing up on the farm in small town Oklahoma I was just a nerd kid with my library card maxed out. I stuttered as a kid from the ages of 5-11. The summer before my sixth-grade year (I was 11) my librarian gave me a book written by an 11-year-old kid. This book changed my life. It's why I'm a writer and book publisher today. I don't remember the name of the book or the title of the book. I just remember there was a watercolor picture of a sailboat on the ocean and that 11-year-old kid steering the boat was the kid that wrote that book. I begin to think, if he can write a book at 11 surely, I can do something with my life. My thinking began to change. Surely, I can do something meaningful with my life. I began to dream. I began to imagine what my life could be like. As the planes flew over our small family farm, I began to say to myself and others who'd listen to me, *"one day I'm going to fly all over the world on planes like that and speak to thousands of people."* And that has truly come to past in the past 30 years to 30 nations and I'm just getting started.

I believe this book has the power to ignite your dreams. I believe this book has the power to help you channel imaginations. I believe this book could potentially help you create a movement that could impact the world in amazing ways even beyond what you've ever imagined.

**There you go, I'm bold enough to say it
are you bold enough to accept it? Buckle up; let's go!**

Michael D. Butler

That being said, there are no guarantees. My formula for achieving Best-Seller Status is designed to work, and it works the majority of the time. There is, however, always the possibility of an unforeseen snag—for example, when 50 people launch a book in your category and genre on the same day you launch. Barring natural disasters, if you do your homework and follow the steps outlined, you should, in fact, achieve your dream: **Best-Seller Status**

Everything Has Changed - Nothing Has Changed

The way that we, as a society, get our information has changed, but consumption of that information has not changed. Who could have imagined in 1979—when I was 11 years old—that we'd have the Internet, Google, Facebook, email, social media, Snapchat, or any of the other modern platforms of communication that we now can't imagine living without?

I remember the encyclopedia salesmen coming by our house every summer. My brother and I were very fortunate. We had encyclopedias and books: shelves and shelves of books. Books from the library, books from church, books we traded with our friends. Books were our life—that and, of course, baseball. Whatever time we didn't spend reading books, we spent trading baseball cards, playing baseball, and dreaming of playing in the big leagues. With only three black-and-white TV channels to choose from—all of which signed off air after the nightly news—reading was our lifeline to the outside world. National Geographic was a favorite—I'll let you guess why.

The 3 Things You Must Have to Go Best-Seller

In this book, I will show you the three things every international best-selling author must know about writing their book, marketing their book, and internationally distributing their book. In the first edition of Best-Seller Status, I provided a basic understand of these three areas of book publishing that can help any author in any genre achieve Best-Seller Status

PART I Writing the Manuscript

PART II Marketing Your Book

PART III Global Distribution

Part IV 52AuthorSecrets.com

Whether you're a fiction or non-fiction author, a first-time author or seasoned author with 20 books under your belt, there are ways to position your book for the global market, increase the likelihood of going best-seller, and sell a ton of books.

Who Can Write a Best-Selling Book?

Everyone's goals are different when it comes to selling books and what they want from increased book sales. I'm confident that, as you cruise through the pages of this book, you'll get a more clearly defined idea of what your goals for your book are and what is truly possible for you.

Perhaps you are an insurance agent or a realtor, and you are looking for more leads and prospects for your business and you want your book to be your digital business card that you can use to add credibility to your brand and do more business. Perhaps you are a new chiropractor, fresh out of chiropractic college and have landed in a new city, where no one knows you, and you need your book to do the same for you. No matter what your career, location, or stage of life, having a book can do all of this for you.

I have a pastor friend who pioneered a church in Phoenix, Arizona two years ago. His goal for writing his book was not about making sales. His book was his vehicle to make an impact in his community, let people know about his church, and help the community to get acquainted with him and his wife.

No matter what your goal is, if you read this book with an open heart and mind, new ideas and thoughts about your purpose will reveal themselves to you, and you will begin writing and communicating at a deeper level.

Embarking on Our Journey to Get You to Best-Seller Status

You are about to get my best content. I'm holding nothing back in the coming pages—I'm going to let you have it all!

The insider secrets I reveal in the pages of this book will help the self-published author just as much as the author with the traditional book publishing deal or with the best Hybrid Publisher—it makes no difference. It has worked for the many people I've shared these secrets with, our own authors at Beyond Publishing, and it will work for you!

As you read, you will, no doubt, discover just how interconnected writing your manuscript, marketing your book, and global distribution are. Just like the organ systems of your body are connected and cannot function unless they work together; writing, marketing, and going best-seller—or, as we like to call, it achieving **Best Seller Status**—all go hand-in-hand. There really is no separating marketing from writing, writing from going best-seller, or marketing from international distribution.

As you see how these three components are interconnected and use them to launch your first best-selling book, your confidence will grow. Soon, you will be cranking out best-sellers on a consistent basis for your loyal friends, fans, and followers.

Definition – Best-Seller Status

Best-seller status is when your book goes #1 on any given recognized best-seller list in your genre category on any given day. There are many best-seller lists, from the New York Times Best-Seller List, to the Wall Street Journal Best-Seller List, to the USA Today Best-Seller List, to the Amazon Best-Seller List. The list of best-seller lists goes on and on. We'll get into more detail on these lists in future editions of this book. Best-seller status is achieved when your book goes #1 on any given recognized best-seller list, on any given day, in your book's category.

By definition, then, choosing the correct category becomes very important. Choosing which category or categories you list your book under in Amazon's system can mean the difference between propelling your book to **Best-Seller Status** and a pile of unread books in your garage.

Why I Live and Work in Los Angeles, California

New York and Los Angeles are the places to be if you want to be in film, television, or publishing. Since I favor L.A.'s weather over New York's, I live in Los Angeles and run my publishing company, Beyond Publishing here. I've since moved the company to Dallas and we are thriving in Frisco Texas.

Los Angeles is famous for people who are trying to become famous. In Hollywood, Beverly Hills, and Santa Monica, it seems that everyone is an actor, writer, producer, or has a job that supports these industries. The smart thing every new actor will do once they arrive in L.A. is to create their official IMDB page and hire an agent. This ensures they can land the most gigs, and, for new actors, if they can land a gig in commercials, they are off to a great start. As an author, you'll need to ask yourself, *What am I the expert at? What do I want to be known for? How do I want Google to index me?*

What New Authors Can Learn from NASA and the Space Shuttle

Exiting the earth's atmosphere takes 80 percent of a space shuttle's fuel. With the remaining 20 percent of its fuel, it can orbit the earth 22 times! So it is with your book, especially your first book. All of the effort, energy, research, writing, and work happens on the front end. But, once you have a successful launch, the residual benefits can really be realized. First, though, you must launch it in the right way, with the right team.

My first book, *Single Dad's Survival Guide* went #1 on Amazon within just a few hours on Father's Day in 2015. I had planned to write Best-Seller Status first, but someone at my company, Beyond Publishing, encouraged me to write *Single Dad's Survival Guide,* and I'm sure glad I followed her suggestion. Based on the fact that there are so many resources for single moms of divorce and very few resources for dads, I was able to capitalize on that and achieve Best-Seller Status very quickly with my book, **The Single Dad's Survival Guide –The Single Dad's Survival Guide: For Re-Connecting with Your Kids & Moving on with Life After Divorce**

That book has sparked a movement, and, as a result, many exciting things are happening. Now that I've given you this preview of what's coming…let's start our main feature and get you and your brand to **Best-Seller Status!**

In this book, I show you the three things every international best-selling author must know about writing their book, marketing their book, and getting international distribution to achieve Best-Seller Status.

PART 1

WRITING YOUR BOOK

The Science of Writing a Best-Seller

Is there a science to writing a Best-Seller? I hypothesize that there is. By looking at the numbers over time, it is easy to see that, in publishing, the best-written books don't always sell the most copies, and poorly written books sell millions. It all comes down to marketing, which we will go into in Part 2: Marketing Your Book.

Many authors have been shocked by the less-than-sophisticated writing quality in *Fifty Shades of Grey*—which sold over 1.25 million copies worldwide and been translated into 52 languages—and the *Twilight* series, which experienced similar numbers, as well as huge box office success. The authors of these books tapped into a niche market and wrote a book that would appeal to those markets. They did not do anything that you can't do—the only difference is that they have gone out there and done it. By the time you finish this book, you will be ready to pursue your own dreams of writing a best-seller.

Robert Kiyosaki, the author of *Rich Dad, Poor Dad*, has said that he aimed to be a *best-selling* author, and that he never proclaimed to be a *best-writing* writer. He has written best-seller after best-seller, and his brand keeps growing with over 30 million books sold.

Give your reader what they want

Even though many of us see our books as our babies, make it about your reader, instead of yourself. People are busy and have less time than ever—distraction is the new norm. To get a readers' attention, you must grab their attention in the first three seconds. From cover design to back cover, to table of contents and sentence structure, it's all about marketing and writing good copy. While it may seem too simplistic, use short sentences, and write at a fifth-grade level, so that it appeals to readers of all types. Many experts have agreed that, unless you're writing a technical manual, authors should write at a fifth-grade reading level. By doing so, you also ensure that your book appeals to readers of all education levels and can sell globally.

Writing your book sounds like the easy part, right? Often, completing the manuscript is the toughest thing for a writer to do.

The process of writing a book can be split into four major phases:

Phase I: Writing the Manuscript

Phase II: Marketing Your Book

Part III: International Distribution and going Best-Seller

Part IV: 52AuthorSecrets.com

Everyone has different goals when it comes to publishing their book, whether they have a message they have to share with the world, a writing talent that can make them wealthy and famous, or a story that they have been writing and rewriting in their minds for years. I'm confident that as you cruise through the pages of this book, you'll get a more clearly defined idea of what your goals are for your book and what is truly possible for you.

• • •

When your mind is racing, it may feel impossible for your fingers to keep up with your brain. What happens when you hit a wall, and it's not you're typing that is the problem?

5 Things that Prevent Authors from Finishing Their Manuscript

- They aren't as passionate about their topic as they thought they were.

- They don't set a deadline for themselves, so other things get in the way, and it never gets done.

- They aren't as knowledgeable as they need to be on the topic, and they don't commit to the research.

- They have too many things going on in their personal life, leading to a lack of focus or commitment.

- They should outsource it or hire a ghostwriter.

Some people are just not good writers. They might be smart in the other 98 percent of their life, but they just get stuck when it comes to writing. Authors who recognize this early can hire a writing coach, learn to leverage tools that help writers, or hire a ghostwriter. Doing so enables them to focus on the other 98 percent of things they *are* good at.

5 Tips to Help New Writers

- *Find a daily time and place to write.* Set a deadline for yourself, and let others know, so you are accountable. If necessary, find a mentor, coach, or accountability partner.

- *Be well-rested and well-nourished.* Sometimes, sleep is all that you need to break through a case of writer's block.

- *Write consistently every day.* Even if it's just a few paragraphs, soon, that will begin to flow into pages and pages. Write at the same place and time each day. When you have a place for your thoughts, the words will flow!

- *Unplug from all distractions. Put your devices on airplane mode, turn off the television, and truly focus on your writing.* It takes over one minute to mentally regain your concentration after you have been interrupted by a text message or other cell phone notification, which means that checking Facebook notifications while you are writing can quickly add up to wasted hours of precious writing time.

- *Learn your best writing style by creating a pattern for yourself and following the suggestions of others to see if it works for you.* Don't get hung up on trying to be the editor, in addition to being the author. You will hire someone to edit your book later. While you are writing, keep the creative juices flowing by staying in the creative side of your brain and letting the thoughts flow.

Mind-Mapping Your Book

Have you ever used a mind-map to brainstorm? Many authors who find themselves stuck in their writing find mind-maps to be an extremely successful method of breaking through their mental barrier and uncovering their best ideas. A mind-map is less limiting and rigid than an outline, and it allows you to mentally form connections between different ideas, without having to try to stuff those ideas into Roman numerals, letters, and numbers. For creative people, like writers, this can be a much more enjoyable and productive process.

There is even free mind-mapping software that can help authors stay organized and visually stimulated. Mind-mapping helps authors connect the threads of a story line or "how-to" series, without leaving out valuable information.

From Book Deal to Movie Deal

Pamala Kennedy is the Author of *MORE THAN RICE – A Journey Through the Underworld of Human Trafficking*, a 196-page book that she wrote in just 15 days. Pamala was motivated by an online contest— she literally felt compelled to pound out the manuscript every morning, starting at 4 a.m., in her sunroom. She felt driven, inspired, and motivated. Not only did she win the contest, her book got picked up by a movie producer in Vancouver, Canada.

As a Former Mrs. California, whose platform was domestic violence, her life was forever changed on a trip to India, where she saw firsthand the evils of human trafficking and how it preyed on children. She felt very passionate about writing her book, giving her the motivation, she needed to power her writing. Years later, she was happy to find her books selling in bookstores in India. We first published her in 2009, and, not only did she realize a lifelong dream of writing her book, she is currently in the process of taking her book to the big screen.

Maybe you're not a morning person, and you can't write for eight hours a day, the way that Pamala did. You have to find what works for you. I've worked with authors who've taken their laptops to work or college and pounded out 20 to 30 minutes of writing on their lunch break, until, one day, the manuscript was complete and ready for editing!

Leverage the Right Tools to Make Writing Easier

In our busy lives, we like to have tools, ranging from productivity apps to email marketing software. For many authors, finding the tools that fit their writing style can mean the difference between publishing in one year and publishing in two years.

I know some authors who still handwrite their manuscript on a yellow legal pad and others who bang it out at an IBM Selectric. Whatever you choose, use what works for you.

Personally, I love to use my publisher in my pocket. That's right: I have a publisher in my pocket, and you have one, too. It's called a smartphone. With my publisher, I can record voicemails, make notes, record video. If I had some good reading glasses and more patience for autocorrect, I could even type my entire manuscript! E.L. James wrote her entire first novel on her Blackberry, and J.K. Rowling's Harry Potter series originated on a napkin!

5 Keys to Help with Completing Your Manuscript

- Leverage tools like your voice recorder on your smartphone. When you sit down at your computer, press *play*.

- Use your smartphone to record video notes to yourself about content to add to your book. I do this all of the time when I'm "hands-free" in the car.

- Dragon Software is dictation software that has helped many authors complete their manuscripts. I haven't personally used it, but several of my author friends love it and swear by it.

- Crowdsource your manuscript. Via social media, you can ask your friends and family to help you write the book. By asking them for feedback or help when you are stuck, they, in essence, help you co-author the book.

- If you get stuck, skip forward and come back to where you were stuck later. Remember doing this when you were taking a test in school? This mental exercise will serve you well.

Sometimes, you just need to take a few hours off or take a few days off, whether you need a break or need to work on another section of your book that you're feeling inspired to write. You'll be refreshed and ready to go when you get back. Often, you will find that it is easy to write what you were struggling with when you come back later.

Writing is Marketing

Writing your manuscript is marketing. It may not feel like marketing when you are writing it, but it is. As an author, you must sell me, the reader, on the idea of why I should keep reading your book and not turn on the TV! Then, you'll need to sell me on the idea of leaving you a 5-star review on Amazon, just like you'll want to do when you are done reading this book.

Most successful authors will tell you they picture the faces of their readers in their mind as they write each sentence. Good authors know what their readers want, but great authors know what their readers are thinking. Careful research is done on the front-end to ensure there is demand for the topic being written, that is a high-ranking search on Google, and that there are few books on the topic.

The simple laws of economics apply when going Best-Seller Status achieving with your book. If a lot of people are searching for your topic and there are not many books on your topic, you may have just struck gold. There is still more research to do, but you are off to a good start if you find the scales of supply vs. demand tipped in your favor.

Do The Research

Maybe hearing the "R word"—research—brings back bad memories of your college or high school days, but, when it comes to writing a best-seller, it is important to do your research. Specifically, it is important to research how many people are searching for your topic of choice on Google every month. Doing so can make you a very wise and wealthy author.

As Abraham Lincoln said, "Give me six hours to chop down a tree, and I will spend the first four sharpening the axe." It is the same with research. The best way to get excited about the idea of research is to think about how it will affect your bottom line. The results can offer some enticing rewards, and not all of them are tied to your bank out—although that certainly is a benefit. If you are like me, it is very satisfying knowing you've helped improve someone's life with your book. The feedback the reviews and the emails an author receives makes it all worthwhile—the money is just an added bonus to invest in marketing and writing a new book.

There are several ways you can do research on your topic, but, in this book, we will cover how to research the demand for your book and how many people are searching for a book on your topic.

Is There Demand for My Book?

In the laws of economics, the simple formula of supply-and-demand is a great way to see if your potential book will be searched for and purchased by book buyers.

Utilize keyword research tools to find out how many searches per month are conducted on your topic.
How many times is your topic searched each month? There are various methods of researching the keywords your readers will use when they search for your book. The one I like most is Google's AdWords platform. Even if you are not purchasing Google advertising, you can utilize the platform to get detailed insights into how your customers are looking for you. By knowing how they will look for you in advance, you can ensure that you will be found by your target audience when you launch your book.

Search Amazon to see how many other books have been written about your topic.
How many books on your topic are in the top 100 list? You can even see which books you can look at for free

or read for free if you are an Amazon Prime member, like I am.

Go to Barnes and Noble.

Search your category and your genre, and study your niche. Bring your smartphone, so that you are able to take some pictures. Make sure that you set aside a few hours, since your research cannot be rushed if you are truly committed to reaching **Best-Seller Status**

If you see a huge demand for a topic while you are doing your research, you can even create a best-selling book on a topic you know nothing about. To do so, you can hire someone to do the research and hire a ghostwriter to write the manuscript. From there, you can use the book to create leads and drive traffic.

The Business of Book Sales

I am a creative. I am a dreamer. I always have been, and I always will be. Being a creative, I had to learn early in my life that being a dreamer, alone—without also being a businessman—could bankrupt me.

Does the sound of business and spreadsheets make you sick, or do you love them? I didn't like Excel spreadsheets until I started reading book royalty payment information about my own book—as well as the books of the authors I work with—

selling in India, Brazil, Europe, Japan, China and all over the world!

Some people operate out of the business side of their brain, and they are good at it. It's like they were born for business and financial success. I was not one of these people.

If you are a creative—and I suspect many of you reading this book are—you can relate to living out of the creative side of your brain. The challenge for us creatives is to listen to the business side of our brains, business partners, or spouses long enough to find success. When you are writing, marketing, and selling your book, it is more important than ever not to ignore the business side of your brain.

How Many Authors Have Written About My Topic?

Doing the research on the front-end can help you hit your target of Best-Seller Status more quickly and efficiently. Someone once told me that if NASA is off just a fraction of a degree on the launch-pad, they could miss their target by millions of miles. Preparation time is never wasted time. Do your research—study market trends, conduct data analysis, and interview of dozens of experts before you settle on a topic and write even the first sentence of your new book.

A huge topic that affects 175 million globally is the health condition endometriosis. When endometriosis sufferer Ania G., from Poland, saw that there was a lack of quality information for women wanting to live well with endometriosis, she decided it was finally time to take the book she had in her heart and put it on paper, so that women worldwide could find hope and information in it. *Alone in the Crowd – Living Well with Endometriosis* was launched, sparking a movement and a life mission for Ania. With many women on multiple continents, she and her staff are able to contribute to the growing conversation of women dealing with this painful disease. She has even captured the attention of celebrities and the medical community. She now has a platform for her message, and she is inspiring a movement across the globe.

Bringing your expertise and passion to a topic that does not have much competition nearly makes you a best-seller before you even start!

The Five Book Genres That Make the Most Money:

For the last ten years, fiction has accounted for roughly 60 percent of book sales, and non-fiction has comprised the other 40 percent. What is not reflected in the

numbers below are self-help, biographies, and how-to books. According to *Publisher's Weekly,* fiction outsells non-fiction at a ratio of 60 to 40. This does not mean that non-fiction does not sell—it absolutely does, as so many of Beyond Publishing's clients are able to attest to. When authors are writing a non-fiction book, they must overcome this gap by making their marketing laser-focused to reach the non-fiction reader. Getting the third-party validation that comes from appearing on television, doing an interview on the radio, or appearing in a top publication plays a large role in make a non-fiction books a success, allowing you to stand out as the expert in your field, far surpassing the credibility of your fellow authors. It's important to know that the slowest moving category of non-fiction books are memoirs and the top selling is "how-to" books.

Which genres sell the most books? Numbers from Nielsen BookScan—which measures and analyzes book sales from around the world—reflect the following:

1. **Romance / Erotica ($1.44 billion).**

2. **Crime / Mystery ($728.2 million).**

3. **Faith-Based / Inspirational ($720 million).**

4. **Science Fiction and Fantasy ($590.2 million).**

5. **Horror ($79.6 million).**

To get a good idea of what is going on in your category, genre, and niche, go to Amazon and search the top 100 titles, based on book sales updated daily, dating back to 1995. https://www.amazon.com/gp/bestsellers/2023/books

You can do the same research at a brick-and-mortar store, like Barnes and Noble or Chapters in Canada. www.chapters. indigo.ca

• • •

The Power of Interviewing Experts to Create a Virtual Stage of Influence

Nothing can make you an expert faster than interviewing other experts.

This is not only an excellent method of gaining credibility, but it builds you an online platform of credibility, before you even launch your book not to mention a ready-made audience of potential book buyers. For those of you who are concerned about running out of content in your book, simply transcribe the video interviews with your experts, and, *voila*, a book!

Read everything there is to read on your topic. Watch every TEDx talk that has been given on your topic and get the equivalent of a PhD on your topic before you begin writing about it. In his book, *Outliers,* author Malcolm Gladwell makes the point that 10,000 hours at anything can make someone an expert in a sport, discipline, or career.

Maybe you're asking yourself, *How can I get an expert to agree to an interview?* Stay tuned, because in Part 2: Marketing Your Book, I will not only show you how, I will go into even more detail on how to harness the power of the interview to leverage Best-Seller Status.

Getting Unstuck

The biggest challenge for new authors is overcoming writer's block, which can hit any author at any time, and it can cause them to get stuck in their book more than once. The average person has 20,000 new thoughts per day. Most of us don't record them, so we forget them.

Your brain may be forming the words far before your fingers are able to type the words, or you may become so overwhelmed by how quickly your mind is racing that you have to take a break from your book until you can calmly write again. Most of the time, writing when our brains are moving too quickly results in ideas that are not fully formed and, sometimes, ideas that don't make sense to anyone later, including the author, themselves.

Alternately, you may find yourself *underwhelmed* by thoughts and struggle to come up with your next chapter. You may even struggle to write your next page, or, worse, your next paragraph. There is no experience that is more disheartening than having to pause in your writing and wait for inspiration. Authors often put a lot of stock in inspiration, but, many times, inspiration is simply fueled by stepping away from the laptop and into the real world, allowing your brain to recharge.

PART II

MARKETING YOUR BOOK

Inevitably, the phone rings on a Monday morning with an excited new author at the other end of the line, ready to be in the *New York Times* as a #1 best-seller. I ask, "When is your book coming out"? They say, "Next week." I wish I could say this doesn't happen, but it does more times than I can count.

If you've done your research, you know you have a hot topic that is in high demand and you've put all of your passion into writing your book, it is time to start marketing your book, so you, too, can achieve Best-Seller Status.

The Seven Ingredients to Market a Best-Seller

A Growing Tribe of Loyal, Raving Fans. It is important that you start building your following on social media and YouTube long before you even consider launching your book. If you wait until launch day to start marketing your book, you will find it very difficult—if not impossible—to catch up. Not only will you not have a ready audience to market to, but you will have had no time to build loyalty. As an author, gaining loyal fans is as valuable as gold.

A ton of free, relevant content being syndicated to those fans on a consistent basis, via video, email, podcasts, blogs and social media. In order to make your launch a success, it is necessary that you nurture your relationship with your fans. Give them new content as often as possible, and stay in touch with them early and often. Get out there on as many channels and platforms as possible—it is not your readers' job to find you; it is your job to come to them.

A growing email list of opted-in subscribers. For marketers, there is nothing more valuable than an email list. Not only does it have more direct ROI (return-on-investment) than any other marketing tool, part of what makes it so valuable is the time that it takes to build. You cannot expect to build a successful email marketing list one week before you launch your book. It takes time, which is why authors start the process two to three years before launching their book.

A growing list of joint venture partners who can help you at book launch time by sharing.

A growing list of online and offline (traditional) media interviews. The media have been the traditional gatekeepers of information, and, as such, readers still trust newspapers, magazines, radio, and television to help them weed through life's clutter and deliver only top-quality information to them. This includes books—viewers know that producers spend a great deal of time selecting which books, products, authors, and experts make it on-air.

Podcasts are the new media. Joe Rogan gets about 11 million listeners on each of his podcast episodes. That is more than the total viewership of the nightly news of all mainstream media combined which is just a few million. Get on sites like podmatch. com and matchmaker.fm early and network your way up into the best podcasts! Start small or where you are and work your way up and do it fast! Podcast interviews are something you can do from your home or office and you can reasonably do 2-10 per day repeating the same content, stories and offers.

While people will get to know you and like you through social media and the content you publish, they already trust their favorite news show and have developed a relationship with their favorite host over many years. While there is never a shortcut to trust, gaining the third-party credibility that getting interviewed or reviewed comes with is like getting a seal of approval.

A Marketing Budget that includes help growing all of your social media—especially Your Podcast Channel. Although you can technically do all of these yourself, chances are that you will not be an expert at all of them, if any of them. Using the platforms incorrectly can lower trust in you and your brand, so you will have to do a great deal of studying before you try to do it all yourself.

Even if you have achieved an expert level of knowledge on marketing your books through all of these channels, do you really want to? It is incredibly time-consuming, and, just when you think you have mastered it all, a new platform emerges or a new update is released that makes everything you thought you knew irrelevant. Publishers, marketers, and publicists are paid to keep up with the latest trends, and they can save you a lot of time—and, perhaps, your sanity.

A hosting platform with you hosting a minimum of 100 podcast interviews or short video segments. The bigger the platform, the better, but accept as many requests for interviews as you can. Interviews do not need to be formal to help you gain attention, credibility, and links back to your website. YouTube,

Blog Talk Radio, iTunes, and other podcast platforms are great places to get your message out to readers.

Staying the Course

A traditional business owner who has developed a thorough business plan doesn't realistically expect to be in positive cash flow for the first five years. If his or her business turns a profit by year five, there is reason for celebration. Why would an author give up too quickly? Many times, when an author quits, it is right before a breakthrough is about to be realized.

Every author we have helped go best-seller over the years has had a 24 to 36-month marketing strategy. An author cannot expect to reach any level of success without having a long-term marketing strategy. Any new business—be it a brick-and-mortar business or an online business—cannot reasonably expect to be in the black and making a profit within the first three years. Only 90 percent of new businesses make it past the first five years. For an author to expect to be a "success" within the first three years is near-sighted, at best.

In the days before Amazon and Google, we used to say in the publishing business that the tipping point for a book going becoming successful was 3,000 books. That is, if we could get 3,000 consumers, book columnists, book reviewers, and book experts talking about the book and sharing it with their friends and family, the book could go viral—even though we didn't talk about "going viral" in those days. In many ways, it feels like the Internet has made us lazier as business owners and authors in many respects, because we expect results easily and more quickly.

Case Study - Chicken Soup for the Soul

Have you heard of Chicken Soup for the Soul? You probably have three or four in your home, right? Chicken Soup for the Soul was rejected by 140 publishers; it is now a two-billion-dollar brand.

When they wrote the Chicken Soup for the Soul series, Jack Canfield and Mark Victor Hansen could have given up after they received those 140 publisher rejections. They were told, "Anthologies don't sell." The series has since sold over 500 million copies. They did not give up and you are not going to give up and I am not going to give up on you either!

Mark Victor Hansen & Jack Canfield

Before social media, getting your story out to the public took some serious effort.

Finishing the manuscript is JUST THE BEGINNING. Now, it's time for the real work to begin! Believing in your message is so profoundly important.

Storytelling Success Equals Sales Success

All good marketers are good storytellers. People don't buy your product until they "buy you." Decide what stories fit your brand and connect you with more of your readers. Then, develop several different versions, based on your audience, the venue, and the time allotted to share with a live audience, on a radio interview or podcast, or your next guest blog post. As you tell compelling, emotionally connecting stories that build relationships with your readers, you'll see book sales follow.

Tell a Compelling Story

Rich Dad Poor Dad

An example of a great storyteller who leveraged his "story" to sell 26 million books is author Robert Kiyosaki.

His fame and revenue allowed him to create a full-fledged business built around his books. He strategically parlayed one success into the next while the books kept cash-flowing his empire, which includes:

- Books
- Seminars
- Board games
- Investments

- Programs
- Speaking
- Consulting
- Venture capital

This is particularly intriguing when you learn that the story of his rich dad and his poor dad was a fable, he created to make a point and to help him connect with his readers. It was not until years later that he revealed it was a parable, a story he created to illustrate a financial point to his listeners and readers.

We all want our stories to go viral. For them to go viral, they must be compelling, authentic, and relatable. It is said that "He or she who tells the best story wins." We all know that being a better writer does not necessarily help you sell more books. Telling a better story will help you be remembered and will help you reach Best-Seller Status faster. Facts tell, but stories sell, and, to make the biggest impact, an author must learn how to tell the best stories.

As a public speaker who has delivered over one thousand keynotes and workshops, 90 percent of the time, I tell the story of how I stuttered as a kid. By doing so, I connect myself with my audience in a way that fosters authenticity, trust, and connection. Many times, I tell my story about being a single dad of four sons, of being a marathoner, or of my son having a bone marrow transplant and overcoming cancer and how his courage and faith inspired thousands. Stories endear us to our audience, make us more human, and create an emotional bond that makes our customers trust us and want to buy from us.

Decide what stories fit in your overall social media story, and weave them in with testimonials, FAQs, and valuable content that educates and entertains your customers. For example, if you're a financial advisor and you write about how to save, choose investments, and minimize risk, tell us stories about clients you've helped, but also tell us why you got into the business of helping people save for retirement. Many times, when an audience or individual hears your 'why', it's just the thing they need to cement that relationship for life! So, tell your story—tell it early, often, and with passion. It will create a lifetime of raving fans ready for your second book, third book, and beyond!

When they were young, my four sons always loved a good story. I'd read to them, take them to the movies, and tell them made-up stories of action and adventure right before bedtime, getting their hearts racing and their imaginations running wild, making it hard for them to go to sleep. To remedy the problem, I'd read another story, and, that time, I would be the one who was falling asleep!

Marketing is not selling; it is sharing. It is a relationship. In **Part I: WRITING YOUR BOOK**, we touched on the fact that all writing is marketing. Now, we're going to go a little deeper.

All marketing is a spiritual transaction. Life is built on the process of exchange. We pay money for things and exchange time for things we value. It's no different when it comes to writing and selling your book. Like an artist who spends hundreds or even thousands of hours painting a masterpiece, as an author, you'll likely spend tens of thousands of hours of writing, researching, and marketing your books in your lifetime. I can't think of a more spiritual thing to do than investing your life in service to others by making your readers' life better in some way. Value the message you have been given, and be a good steward of your message by delivering it faithfully to your friends, fans, followers, and readers. It is a great blessing and a great responsibility to deliver the message you have as clearly and as powerfully as possible.

The Power of the Interview

One of my favorite forms of communication is the interview. Although I don't have a broadcasting degree, one way I overcame stuttering as a child was hosting my own television talk show on my family's farm in northeastern Oklahoma. I was the producer, the host, and the guest—I'd even read the commercials when we'd take a station break. Neither my brother nor the cows would hear me stutter at all for a full half-hour. It was all pretend, but by tapping into my imagination I was able—with God's help—to overcome my stuttering.

Fast-forward to today. In my adult years, I've been able to interview some amazing people, including: Governor Mary Fallon, business icon Brian Tracy, movie producers, university presidents, and dozens of amazing authors with incredible stories. The thing I like about the interview format is that it provides a wealth of content for authors who want to start their process by having their interviews transcribed. Done right, interviews come off as a relaxed conversation, require little preparation, and make the audience feel at ease.

A 15-minute interview can provide ample content for a short book—approximately 5,000 words or up to 20 pages. For a new author who is trying to create content, this can be huge. Beyond that, the footage can provide a great video that can be used to promote the book.

Getting the Top Person on Twitter to Mention You Twice

Early on, I promised that I would answer the question, "How do I get the expert or celebrity to notice me and give me the interview?" In the late 2000s, my PR Firm was doing some free work for a non-profit I'm very fond of helps rescue kids who are trafficked for sex to get the traffickers prosecuted.

At the time, Ashton Kutcher had the largest Twitter following on all of Twitter, with about 12 million followers. He was only putting out about one tweet a day back then, and having him tweet us was like having a 30-second spot on all the major new outlets in primetime! Twitter lists were big back then, too, so he listed our non-profit in two of his top lists of trafficking organizations and mentioned us in two tweets on a single day! How did we get that exposure? By simply asking. We sent him a few tweets, and, *bam*, we got what we wanted! It is all a matter of asking the right person at the right time. Of course it didn't hurt that the popular movie, **TAKEN**, came out about that time and was doing really well at the box office and educating people on the dark side of human trafficking.

Public Relations Book Strategy

We saw similar success with many of our other clients, like getting all of the local news networks to turn out for a Human Trafficking Awareness Day press conference. It's really just a matter of contacting the right reporter or news anchor who is covering the right "beat" or subject matter.

For example, if you're launching a book in the health and wellness category, get a national press release syndicated, then, contact your local newspaper, TV, and radio station with the news. Be sure you contact the health editor or reporter with your news, and you are more likely to get airtime, especially if you tie your story to a health awareness day on the editorial calendar, which has meaning to the editor or producer and their audience, rather than just being about your book launch. If you can help them fill dead air space and do their work for them, they'll invite you back again and again.

If your book is about childhood obesity, you might donate 30 books to the moms of students at one of your local schools who struggle with obesity and do a free cooking clinic with healthy recipes. With such a compelling hook, the local TV station will be more likely to come out and do a story. By doing something positive in the community, you won't be seen as another author just trying to hawk your book.

Social Media Marketing is Not New

Social media is not new. It has been around since the dawn of time. Humans have always been social, and we've always used media to share our message. In Ancient Greece the Spartans would run up to 70 miles per day to deliver an urgent message, and, later, Native Americans used smoke signals to communicate.

In modern times, we have communicated through methods that are increasingly more advanced: telegraph, telephone, radio, television, and, now, the myriad of ways that we use computers, the Internet, and smartphones to share our message. The goal of our communication on social media should not be to broadcast our sales message, but, rather, to inspire a conversation in the public arena around other people getting educated about our product and becoming evangelists for our brand.

How to Leverage Social Media in the Internet Age to Sell More Books

Like the printing press bringing us out of the Dark Ages, the Internet is revolutionizing the publishing industry, giving new authors an unprecedented opportunity.

Fact #1: Authors who learn how to leverage social media and the Internet with an online community will sell more books and gain more fame.

Fact #2 Most authors do not know how to correctly use social media, and, instead, of helping their brand, they actually hurt their brand.

7 Simple Steps to Getting it Right with Social Media and Selling More Books as an Author

1. Brand Your Name

Fiction authors, non-fiction authors, self-help authors, and faith-based authors can all benefit by branding their name. One of the first things that you should do when you are branding your name is to purchase your domain name. If yourname.com is not available, you may want to add a middle initial, like I did with MichaelDButler.com.

By owning your URL yourname.com, you can keep your fans and readers hooked with your blog, building an audience

you can leverage each time you write a new book. You will also want to brand your name on all social media channels by creating a pretty permalink for each of the sites, rather than keeping the randomized permalink that is assigned to you, personalize it with your actual name. (i.e., Facebook.com/yourname, Linkedin.com/yourname, etc.). This will make it easier for fans to find you and follow you and, over time, it will give you tremendous search engine boost.

2. Brand Your Face

Having a close-up, current headshot will serve you well in the long run. You may love your dog, your grandkids, or your automobile, but people want to connect with you, the author, which is why a photo of your face is preferable to one of your pets. People buy from us when they know us, like us, and trust us, and nothing helps that happen faster than a current profile picture that is consistent across all social media channels.

Since the majority of social media is accessed from smartphones, it is important to make it easy for people to recognize you by using a consistent, easy-to-see, and easy-to-share photo of your face. Use the same photo on Facebook, Twitter, Instagram, Pinterest, your Website, Podcast channels, LinkedIn, YouTube, and all other social media channels.

3. Leverage Your Keywords Across Multiple Social Media Channels

The Internet gives us the opportunity to connect with potential joint venture partners by leveraging keywords online. For example, if I'm a self-help author, it is very beneficial for me to connect with other self-help authors on social media. This will not hurt my book sales. This will allow others who are following them to find me, providing value for both of us.

We've seen it happen again and again in every genre of books: authors who are not threatened by "competition" end up winning in the long run. We've even seen two of our authors land movie deals as a result of leveraging their keywords on social media platforms and getting others to talk about them. This third-party credibility caused a production company to take notice and take action!

4. Hire Experts and Use Tools

There are a number of free and fee-based tools to help authors find potential joint venture partners online and sell more books. Hootsuite.com and Twiends.com are two of my favorites. A Google search or a search on Mashable. com will show the latest and most reputable tools for managing your brand online.

Experienced authors who are getting royalty checks should consider outsourcing part or all of their social media to a qualified agency. It is more affordable than many authors realize, and it can free up more time for the author to do what they are good at and what produces the most income: writing more books. Outsourcing one's social media does not make it less personal. Any qualified agency will take the necessary time to get to know the core message of the author and ensure that the message, content, and personality of the writer comes through in all online interactions.

5. Get Others to Talk About You and Your Books

Third-party validation is incredibly powerful when it comes to online buying. This is why creating a relationship with potential joint venture partners is huge. An author who only talks about himself or herself will lose followers, but those who brag on others will find that others naturally want to brag on them, too. 'Go-Givers Gain' when it comes to broadcasting online. Learn the 25% Rule of Engagement: talk about yourself only 25 percent of the time and talk about industry news and facts, humor, FAQs, and experts in your niche the other 75 percent of the time. You will soon find those same experts esteem you as a colleague and begin sharing your stuff freely. One surefire way to ensure others won't keep talking about you is by ignoring or not replying to FAQs and online sharing. Utilize free monitoring software to track when others are talking about you and your book online, so you can thank them and return the favor. Once again, I love hootsuite.com for this.

6. Have a Winning Content Creation Strategy That Includes Video

The fastest way for your content to go 'viral' is to have it on video. Since Google owns YouTube, and 75 percent of search results are based on video content, you will be miles ahead of others in your field if you focus on video marketing for the next five years. If you want people to share your content, make it shareable. Use social media buttons like http://wordpress.org/plugins/addthis/. If you're following our 25% Rule of Engagement formula we mentioned above, you can feel confident in asking people to retweet and share your content across all their social media channels.

7. Repurpose Your Content

There is nothing lazy about repurposing content; it is smart! Content is king on the Internet, and, to get found, you must have new and fresh content on a weekly basis. To get found, indexed, and shared, you must constantly share quality content.

Growing up on the farm, I loved eating my mother's cooking. She always made something delicious, nutritious, and enjoyable, but she only used the same four food groups over and over. Many times, she mixed a new dish with leftovers from the day before.

You can apply this same principle in your content creation strategy. For example, every one of the numbered points in this book chapter originated as a YouTube video, blog post, or a series of tweets, Facebook posts, and Google+ posts.

The easiest way to create content is to shoot a weekly video from some of the FAQs we get from our clients. After shooting the video, I type up the manuscript from the video and post this text along with the video on my YouTube channel and my blog. In fact, YouTube helps you out by giving you the transcript (you will want to edit it however it's not perfect, especially if you have an unusual accent.) Now, I have a search-engine-optimized piece of valuable content that will drive traffic to me, based on what we do for authors and I make it shareable using: http://wordpress.org/plugins/addthis/ and tweet it, share it on Facebook, and post it on Google+, Pinterest, and the social bookmarking sites, like Reddit, StumbleUpon, Digg, and Delicious.

Twitter Marketing

Twitter is like the broad side of a funnel. It is designed to attract a tribe based on your interests and move potential buyers through your relational maze of all things *you* at YourName.com.

Twitter is like a rock concert. It is loud, noisy, and there are people puking their information on you.

Twitter is not meant for "meaningful conversation"—it is not even like a first date. Twitter is like bumping into someone in a crowded elevator and exchanging business cards, opening up the door to a larger conversation via email, phone call, or face-to-face appointment.

The entire goal of Twitter is: "If you like me on Twitter, connect with me on my website or Facebook." Twitter is one of my favorite social media platforms as an author, because it so quickly gets authors indexed by Google. Since it's a micro-blogging platform, it serves the same function of a blog headline in getting indexed by search engines more quickly.

Search Engine Optimization and YouTube

This is very useful since there is so much new information showing up on Google daily that the search engines have trouble indexing all this massive content daily and topically,

search engines like Google, Bing, and Yahoo depend heavily on Google and YouTube to topically sort and present the information to us the consumers in a logical fashion. The real kicker here is with the right training you, as the author, can learn how much time and money we were wasting before we knew how to leverage Google's search engines.

Can I #Hashtag my way to Bestseller Status?

The hashtag # has been popular since Twitter launched in 2006, and it has spread to other social media platforms, like Facebook and Instagram. Users and search engines are able to utilize hashtags to index topics or relevant keywords. Just as doing one bench press cannot make you an Olympic Gold medalist, one hashtag, alone, cannot make you a best-selling author.

Hash-tagging your way to success won't happen without tens of thousands of them. Likely, you will need a far more robust marketing strategy, but, if you understand how a hashtag can help Google index you and help readers find you, you are far ahead of the pack.

A Penny Doubled Daily for 30 Days or $200,000 Cash?

My mentor asked me 20 years ago if I'd rather have a penny doubled daily for 30 days or $200,000 cash? I'm not very good at math, but I quickly grabbed my calculator and did the math.

Achieving Best-Seller Status is a lot like this concept. It's the synergistic energy that comes together the last few days of the book launch that makes everything "somehow magically happen" as one new author put it.

It might not look like a lot is happening on the social media side of things, and, perhaps the PR strategy is not making the phones ring right away. Don't fret. If you're working the Best Seller Status System, it *will* work for you. By the way, a penny doubled daily for 30 days is $5,368,709.12, and, on day 31, you'd rake in a whopping $10,737.418.24!! Wow over 10 million dollars! Aren't you glad you did not quit? Everyone else may have given up on your but you are not going to give

up on you and I'm not going to give up on you either! The world needs to hear your story!

What if your marketing budget was $10,737.418.24? What percentage would you invest in your brand and your future book sales?

In looking at the above question, my answer is that you would invest the same percentage into your brand and book sales as you are right now. The tipping point is different for every genre. As long as you follow the prescribed formula, the "magic" will happen for you! It's like getting up every day and going to work and going to the gym. You might not want to. You probably don't feel like it, but you do what you have to do to get the results you want.

You know that while you are working and being consistent, your competitor is taking shortcuts or calling in sick. You'll be ready to win and win big on launch day, and you'll feel good about the fact that you did not cheat. You were true to yourself and to your core life message and brand. You showed up. You did what

God asked you to do, and you touched thousands of lives as a result of it. Now that is a good feeling, isn't it?

Business at the Speed of Trust

It is true that people do business with those they know, like, and trust. It's especially true when it comes to buying you and buying your books. While potential buyers of your book will require less time to research you and your message when spending $15.95 to $24.95 for your book than when buying a car, house, or vacation home, the need to establish rapport, trust, and confidence in you as the messenger are still very much important.

Is it easier to sell one of your books to a consumer online who you've never met or to sell 2,000 of your books by negotiating with an HR manager who needs to bring you in as an author to speak on improved teamwork and job performance? By creating the persona, you want online and being consistent with your brand and your core life message, over time, people will feel like they know you, and, indeed, they do.

Business will happen faster than you could have imagined, all because you took the time and made it easy for people to get to know the authentic you and your core life message. When that message resonates with a person, an audience, or an entire market, it is truly golden. When that happens, it is time to write book number two, create a workbook, and package a coaching program around your book!

Getting others talking about you and your book on social media is truly the greatest example of Getty's vision that I know.

PART III

PUBLISHING AND GLOBAL DISTRIBUTION

We now come to the true payout for all of your efforts. Perhaps you spent years writing your book and months marketing your book. Now, we come to the part where you actually get paid for your efforts.

Types of Publishing

In the past, authors only had one real choice when it came to publishing: send their manuscript to dozens of publishers and hope that the phone will eventually ring. In this day and age, authors have a variety of options to choose from, which, while liberating, can be confusing to a new author.

Self-Publishing

Publishing your book on your own with CreateSpace or Lulu. The upside is that you don't share royalties with the publisher, but you don't get broad distribution. It is more difficult to get into bookstores and libraries, and navigating international distribution can be like learning how to build your house or fix your car on your own.

Traditional Publishing

Having a publisher do all of the work and make all of the investment. Before the Internet, this was primarily reserved for A-list celebrities and people with huge followings, like Oprah Winfrey or Joel Osteen. The downside is that the royalty payouts typically range from 7 to 25 percent, and the publisher typically keeps the rights to the book. The upside to you is that all of the logistical details are handled by the publisher.

Hybrid Publishing

The hybrid model of publishing is fairly new. It combines the best of the self-publishing and traditional publishing models to give an author full control, while sharing the expense for startup to make the royalty payout closer to 50 percent. In this type of publishing, the publisher handles the logistics of the book distribution, including: bookstores, libraries, and international distribution. The author keeps the rights to the book, including subsequent movie rights.

These are your choices, but, for the author, there are many other things to consider prior to publishing that we have not yet addressed. In order to make an educated decision, you will need to have a basic understanding of what goes into taking a book from conception to publication, including: editing, ghostwriting, book cover, eBook conversion, interior layout, ISBN number, Library of Congress number, and translation. At Beyond Publishing we offer Hybrid Publishing because it is best for authors in most cases. Every case is different. Why not reach out to us and let us look at your book and have our team give you some thoughts on your manuscript and launch strategy based on your goals for your book.

English is required learning in for all years of elementary school in China, making Mandarin and English the top two languages in all of the world. When you are writing and marketing your book, remember that you will be touching a global audience with your message.

Get ready to take your book global. It's sooner and easier than you might think.

Before you finish your book, there are a few more things that you will need to consider:

Editing

There are different types of editing, and it can be difficult to determine what the differences are. Even amongst editors, not all of them can agree on a single definition of an edit.

Copy editing

A copy editor will ensure that your book is grammatically correct before it goes to print. Although we recommend line editing to all of our authors, a copy edit by someone author than your spouse. Too many authors assume that their friends and family will catch their mistakes and "let them know"— even if

they did catch them; would they really want to hurt your feelings by telling you? They may have caught a few mistakes, but chances are that not only were they not qualified to edit your book, they also didn't want to tell you just how many mistakes they found as a casual reader. By making a few small suggestions, they prove that they read your book, without overwhelming you with negative feedback. The truth is that, without an editor, you will get negative feedback, but it will be very public.

Line editing

If copy editing is about ensuring that you don't look bad, line editing is about making sure that you look good. An editor will correct your book for flow, sentence structure, word choice, and more.

Developmental Edit

In a developmental edit, an editor will not only make sure that your writing is error-free from a grammatical standpoint, but they will also help you with areas your book needs to improve, from character development to pace.

Ghostwriting

Ghostwriting is a process that is different for everyone. While some people really do outsource the entire job of writing their book, most authors want some part in the writing process. Many ghostwriters conduct a series of

interviews with an author, from which they are able to write sections of the book and develop new questions for their next interview session.

Book Cover

People may be urged not to judge a book by its cover, but let's face it, we do. Having a professional cover is one of the most important steps that you can take in marketing your book. There is nothing that makes an author look more amateurish than having a dated, sloppy, or boring book cover.

E-Book Conversion

E-Book conversion takes your book from a file on your computer to a format that is readable on all platforms. Epub3 is the global industry standard.

Interior Design

You may not think about all of the work that is put into a book while you are reading it, but publishers put a great deal of thought into chapter headings, fonts, locations of page numbers, pull-out quotes, graphics and text boxes and more. If you try to take a book straight from a document to Kindle it will be noticeably unprepared for market.

ISBN number (International Standard Book Number)

An ISBN number is like a barcode. It helps readers from around the world identify your book and indexing organizations index it topically.

Library of Congress Number

Much like an ISBN number, a Library of Congress number allows readers to locate you within the Library of Congress's vast collection. Having a proper Library of Congress and ISBN can make it easier to get your book into libraries, bookstores and global distribution.

Translation

If you have a following in another country, as Ania G. did in Poland, it is important to have a translation of your book in the language spoken in that country. As your book's popularity grows, demand for translation into more and more languages will grow.

Book Category

The category that your book is in can be incredibly broad, like "general fiction", to very specific. The more specific that you can get with your category, the better that you are able to target your ideal readers, helping you to go best-seller.

Life Cycle of a Book

The life cycle of a book is the journey that a book takes from conception to launch to *Best Seller Status* to your book offered as a customized coaching program.

P.O.D.

Print on Demand is a method of printing physical copies of books that helps authors avoid losing their guestroom to copies of their book that never sold. In this method of printing, authors wait until they need a quantity of books and print them as necessary. Authors must weigh the financial cost of purchasing a small quantity—which is more expensive per book—with the risk of purchasing a large quantity. It is important to know your market very well before you decide how many print copies you should order.

Subtitle

The subtitle of a book gives a more in-depth explanation of what your book will be about. In the past, the subtitle was all about catching a reader's attention with a few words that explained why it was important to them (titles don't always make the topic of the book evident). Today, it does that on a much more evolved scale: it utilizes keywords to help your book get found online.

While all of this may seem overwhelming, it is a formulaic process that can be replicated time and again to launch best-seller after best-seller. Once you have been through the process the first time, you will soon be listing yourself as a "3-Time Best-Selling Author"—or even more—in your professional bio.

Thank you for investing in yourself by reading *BOOK IDEA TO BESTSELLER*

I believe the world is truly waiting for your book. I believe you have a message that is so special and unique that only you are able to deliver it to the world, exactly as it should be delivered, and precisely as it has been stamped on your heart by the fingerprint of God. As you obey your inner urge to share your message with the world and move forward on this path, the world will thank you for opening up your heart by opening up to you. Like a painter using oil on the canvas, your words will transform someone's life, and, in the process, you will be inspired to give again. In doing so, you have the power to uplift, entertain, and inspire your readers, all because you chose to follow your heart and share your soul. And even more of the world heard about what you did, because you humbly accepted the title that was given to you: ***BEST-SELLER STATUS***!

Congratulations for making it this far, now we're ready to get you Q'd up for the Best-Sellers Lists! Let's dive into Part 4 based on my popular video series 52AuthorSecrets.com based on my top questions received from new authors around the world. With authors in 64 nations, millions of book sales and nearly 1,000 titles published at the time of this release November 2023. You can watch them all at 52AuthorSecrets.com and enjoy reading them here. Applying most of these that fit for your personality and book genre can make you highly successful as an author! Let's go!

Author's Note: This next section was transcribed from my popular video series 52AuthorSecrets.com transcribed from my videos around the world so when you see the locations of London, Dubai, Greece or Jerusalem, etc...in the content you'll know where I am in the world when I was first sharing this content.

Let's go......

PART IV

52AuthorSecrets.com
THE 52 FAQS OF AUTHORS GLOBALLY

Secret #1 Have Fun

If you're an author and you're writing a book, it's so important to have fun. Let the enthusiasm with your writing come through. One of the best ways I do this, whether I'm writing fiction or nonfiction, once I figure out who my reader is, is I close my eyes and I think about the reader.

And I look into their eyes. I look at their face, and I see their face light up as they're reading my book. As I'm sitting at my computer and I'm typing so fast, it's like we're having a two-way communication. I can hear what they're thinking. I can hear the questions they're asking.

Have fun and let the enthusiasm come through. It'll make a difference, and your reader will notice. And they'll think, this author really cares about me. They'll feel the love. They'll feel the fun. And they'll take action!

Most importantly, fiction or nonfiction, have fun and listen. Maybe writing is not your thing. It's okay. Hire a ghostwriter. But make sure your ghostwriter knows how to have fun with you and your reader.

If you're going to be an author, have as much fun as possible!

When you're having fun work feels like play. Sweat = success, long hours become joyful and alarm clocks are not necessary. Live with joy and change the world with your book!

Secret #2 Do the Research

Start by figuring out what you want to achieve with your research. Think about the specific areas or questions you want to explore in your book. Dive into different sources to gather information. Look for books, articles, websites, interviews, documentaries, or even real-life stories that relate to your chosen topic. Don't limit yourself—explore as much as you can!

Head to physical or online libraries and archives to access a wealth of knowledge. You'll find books, journals, historical records, and other valuable resources that can deepen your understanding of your subject. Make the most of search engines by using different keywords and advanced search techniques related to your book's topic. Look for reliable websites, digital libraries, academic journals, or databases to find relevant information.

Reach out to people who have expertise or experience in your book's subject. Interviewing them can provide unique insights, personal stories, or expert opinions that will make your content richer.

Consider attending conferences, seminars, or workshops related to your topic. You'll have the opportunity to learn from experts, connect with professionals, and stay updated on the latest research and developments. Join online forums, social media groups, or professional communities where discussions about your book's topic take place. Participate actively, ask questions, and gain insights and perspectives from others. As you conduct research, keep organized notes. Jot down important points, interesting facts, and sources to cite later. This will help you stay organized and ensure accurate referencing.

Double-check the information you gather by cross-referencing it with multiple sources. It's crucial to ensure that the facts, statistics, and claims you include in your book are accurate and reliable. Use digital tools like note-taking apps or cloud storage to keep your research materials in order. Create folders or labels to categorize your information and easily find what you need later.

Remember, as an expert on your chosen topic, you bring valuable knowledge and insights to your book. Research serves to enhance and strengthen your understanding, filling in any gaps and providing additional perspectives.

Secret #3 Discover Your Why

Decide why you want to write your book. Do you want your book to create credibility for you? Get you on stages? Get you media and podcast interviews? The number one reason an author writes a book is to establish credibility in their industry as a thought leader. Begin your book with the endgame in mind. Where is the destination? Where do you want to go? Do you want to take the scenic route or the superhighway?

In a moment we'll talk about the strategy and business plan for your book but now, let me know your why! Maybe you're writing to educate, perhaps you're becoming an author to entertain with humor, fiction, or poetry. Are you trying to persuade an audience to act? The more time you spend on your why, the greater impact and reach the finished book will have. Abraham Lincoln said, *"if I had six hours to chop down a tree, I'd spend the first four sharpening my axe."* Now is the moment to get laser focused on what this first book for you will be. Don't try to put three book ideas into one book, only present one laser focused idea or central theme otherwise you'll miss making the impact you could.

Secret #4 Discover Your Avatar

Just like these building behind me on the beach in Dubai, your book needs a blueprint too, and that starts with knowing your avatar and your purpose.

Once you have identified your target audience and clarified your goals for the book, you can align your writing and marketing strategies accordingly. Understanding your avatar will help you tailor your content to their specific needs, interests, and preferences. It will guide your choice of language, examples, and storytelling techniques.

Having a clear focus will also help you structure your book effectively. You can organize your chapters, sections, and topics in a way that appeals to your target audience and delivers your message in a coherent and engaging manner. By knowing your avatar, you can address their challenges, provide solutions, and offer valuable insights that resonate with them.

Additionally, being focused allows you to streamline your marketing efforts. You can identify the most relevant platforms, communities, and channels to promote your book to reach your ideal readers. Whether it's speaking engagements, media appearances, or online advertising, your understanding of your avatar will guide your decisions on where and how to market your book effectively.

Remember, writing a book is not just about sharing your knowledge or story; it's about connecting with your readers and making an impact. The power of focus lies in creating a book that speaks directly to your avatar, addresses their needs, and helps you achieve your desired outcomes as an author.

To write a bestselling fiction or nonfiction book, it's crucial to have a deep understanding of your reader and who your avatar is. You need to know what they are currently engaged with, what podcasts they listen to, and which authors and books they are reading. This knowledge will significantly impact your writing and marketing strategies once you have identified your target demographic.

For example, let's consider my target reader: a woman over 40 who has recently transitioned in corporate life and has just delivered a compelling TED talk. Although she doesn't have a book yet, she aspires to make a positive impact on the world. This specific niche represents one of our three primary targets. As an author, it's important to identify and empathize with your reader's unique characteristics.

Think about the country they reside in, their preferred tooth paste brand, their educational background, their income level, and even the TV shows they enjoy watching. Understanding these details will allow you to connect with your avatar on a deeper level. When writing your book, start with the end in mind by considering what your reader wants to read and what they are currently seeking.

By tailoring your book to their preferences, you will create a stronger appeal and engage your avatar more effectively. This approach involves writing the book backwards, meaning you

align your content with what your reader desires and what they are looking for at this moment.

Remember, capturing the interest and attention of your reader begins with understanding their tastes, interests, and desires. By immersing yourself in their world, you can create a book that resonates with them on a personal level and ultimately meets their needs.

Secret #5 Maintain Creativity as an Author

To stay creative and focused throughout the writing process, it's essential to prioritize and nurture your creative side. Avoid slipping into editing mode prematurely, as it can hinder your creativity. The brain is divided into two hemispheres: the creative side and the analytical side. When you shift into editing mode, you engage the analytical side and risk dampening your creative flow.

Experts have long emphasized the importance of staying in creative mode while writing. By doing so, you allow your ideas to flow freely without the constraints of self-criticism and analysis. Instead of editing as you write, focus on generating and capturing your ideas. Embrace the freedom to explore different possibilities, experiment with narrative techniques, and unleash your imagination onto the pages.

Remember, your primary goal during the initial writing phase is to unleash your creativity and bring your story or message to life. By staying in creative mode, you can maintain a laser focus on crafting a dynamic and exciting book that will captivate your readers.

When it comes to editing, it's advisable to seek the assistance of a professional editor. They possess the expertise to provide an objective evaluation of your work, ensuring that it meets the highest standards. Collaborating with an editor allows you to maintain your role as the creative force behind the book while benefiting from an outside perspective that enhances the overall quality of your work.

As an author, your energy and efforts should primarily be directed toward harnessing your creativity and producing an engaging manuscript. Trust in the editing process and the expertise of professionals to refine your work. This way, you can focus on what you do best; writing and staying connected to your creative flow.

By embracing your creative side and leaving the editing to the experts, you position yourself to become a truly accomplished author.

Today I'm in Costa Rica teaching a mastermind on how to write a book. But you don't have to get out of your country or even get out of your state. Just get out of your house sometimes.

Go for a walk, go to the park, even hey, go to the mall. Anytime you change the scenery, you reroute the synapses of your brain. It doesn't matter if you're writing fiction or nonfiction.

It helps you come up with a better product and get better ideas. During the pandemic, I encouraged people to get in their car, go for a drive, and write in the car. Whatever it is, do something different. Take your dog for a walk and write while you're at the park. Maybe even write on the notes feature of your phone and then come back and import it into your computer.

Get creative. The world will be better because you did get out. Expand your vibe and you'll expand your flow.

Secret #6 The Power of Focus

An average of 2.1 hours are lost daily as a result of distractions

One way that I combat distractions is I write at the same time each day. My best time is five in the morning. It's quiet then, my email and phone are not blowing up. That might not be the best time for you to write. Your best time might be late at night or in the middle of the day. Whenever it is figure it out and stick to it. Writers who write at the same time and the same place each day begin to anticipate the creativity and their subconscious mind begins to produce the endorphins for writing at those times each day. The mind and body can be trained to write more effectively over time. Research is starting to prove this as well.

Are you writing your book to get more credibility? Whatever the reason is, be very laser focused on if your client is a woman over 40 or if it's men in high school and college. Who is your avatar? Who is your reader?

All these things are going to go into how focused you get and what chapters and what sentences you write. Don't write a single word until you know exactly who your target market is and what you want the book to do for you. You see some beautiful buildings around me, and they were all blueprints and plans on a draftsman's desk in an architectural firm before they were ever built. Everything worthwhile begins with laser focus!

Secret #7 Become a Better Writer by Increasing Your Endorphins

Do you get stuck when it's time to write your chapter? I want to encourage you write at the same time every day, like going to the gym. Your endorphin levels will increase, your anticipation will increase after you get past that writer's block of pain, of just getting up and doing it. Half of the battle is just showing up at the gym. Half of the battle is just showing up at your computer to write. Write at the same time every day. And even if it's just 500 words, give yourself props if it's just 15 minutes, give yourself time to write. Give yourself space, like you do for a meal or your meditation. Give yourself space to write, and the creative ideas will come. Start flexing that muscle. Start flexing that muscle and begin using that writing muscle.

Secret #8 Write Every day to Get Better

Just like going to the gym, you've got to do it every day. And if you want to knock your book out in a timely manner to change the world and create a movement, you want to get laser focused.

I know it sounds like I'm repeating myself but of all the writing I've done since age 11 this is the most valuable advice I can share.

You feed yourself three meals a day, right? You go to the gym every day. Why not write every day and exercise that muscle to create a winning masterpiece? Most of all, have fun. That's what I'm going to do!

Secret #7 Know WHY You Are Writing

This is one of the most important parts. Start with why. When you start with why the how and the what become easy. Why are you writing this book? For more credibility? To get more speaking events? To get more podcast interviews? To fill up your mastermind? When you're crystal clear on your why the how and the what become easy.

Before you write a single word, before you pen a single sentence, before you sit down at the computer, do your research, know who your avatar is, do a deep dive and know what it is you want to accomplish. Do you want to entertain? Do you want to educate? Do you want to inform? Do you want to cause massive action? Do you want to create a movement? Or do you just want to entertain with fiction and give somebody some fiction to read before they go to bed at night? Do your research. Know exactly what it is you want to accomplish. That way, you're always in charge when the book becomes a movie and the movie changes lives with your movement.

Do you want to create a course from your book, perhaps a workshop or a keynote or a platinum coaching program you could charge tens of thousands for? Think of the book as the wide end of the funnel to capture your actual target market. Perhaps your target is not just a reader who'll spend $30 on your book but a client who'll spend $50,000 for your coaching for one year, how would that make you feel?

Recently one of our author clients' named Seth acquired a new client to his financial services business by giving away a free $25 book. The client brought a portfolio worth $200 million to my client's financial firm. I said, *"Seth are you going to keep giving out free books?"* You can guess what the answer was!

Secret #8 Have a Business Plan for Your Book

You know, a lot of authors are playing checkers when it comes to strategy, I recommend playing chess because you always want to be thinking five moves ahead. It's not just about launching the book next month, it's about everything that goes into it. Your joint venture partners lined up, preselling the eBooks, preselling the print book. What is your launch date?

Do you have speaking, and podcast interviews lined up? I'm going to say, if you're not playing chess with your book strategy and book launch, others are going to be saying to you, checkmate. And so, get on my calendar right MeetwithMichaelD.com talk to my staff, talk to me. We're going to help you get published properly. Michael D from Dubai today, and you'll be the one in the driver's seat saying: check mate!

Secret #9 The Power of UNPLUGGING to FINISH YOUR Book

Have you ever heard of the saying, *"can't see the forest because of all of the trees"*? That's how it can be in the third phase of writing. You've developed a good strong idea to write about, you've done your research and created the outline, now you're up to your neck trying to pull everything together and not leave anything out, this is the overwhelm phase. This is a normal phase and the BEST time for you to UNPLUG! *"Unplug"* you ask, *"but my book is almost finished!"* Yes indeed, this is the exact time you need to unplug and take two steps back, take a breath, take a trip, go on a vacation, and revisit your manuscript when you return. Your mind will thank you; your family will thank you and most importantly your reader will thank you! What comes out of your heart and mind at this phase as you put the icing on the cake is pure gold. This is like giving the stew in the crock pot a few more hours to simmer, it makes all the difference, and the reader is impacted 100x more by it! Unplug, recharge, reignite then finish that bestseller!

And take a break. That's right. If you've been writing hard, it's like working. Working the brain, working the mind, working the heart and soul on writing that book. Unplug and guess what? I'm going to be ready to write tomorrow morning. So, unplug. Take a break. In sports growing up, the coach had us run wind sprints. It's more effective to do short bursts of running fast than to try to do a marathon. And you're going to find you're much more effective in your writing. I write 15 minutes at a time. That's my tip today. Take a break. Enjoy unplugging. Don't feel guilty about enjoying life. Your book will get done quicker.

Secret #10 Using ChatGPT and AI to Organize Book Chapters and Generate Writing Ideas

Chatgpt and AI can be valuable tools in organizing your book chapters and generating writing ideas. Here's how you can leverage their capabilities:

1. Brainstorming and Idea Generation:
    - Engage in a conversation with ChatGPT, discussing your book's subject, themes, and goals. Describe what you want to achieve with each chapter or section.
    - Ask ChatGPT for suggestions and prompts related to specific topics or themes you want to cover in your book.
    - Use AI-powered writing tools or platforms to generate ideas and prompts based on keywords or concepts related to your book's content.

2. Outlining and Chapter Organization:
    - Collaborate with ChatGPT to create an outline for your book. Discuss the main points, subtopics, and chapters you envision.
    - Seek AI assistance in structuring your chapters by discussing the logical flow of ideas, arranging sections, and determining the order of topics.
    - Utilize AI-powered tools that provide templates or frameworks for organizing book chapters. These tools can suggest different structures and help you visualize the overall organization.

3. Research and Fact-checking:
    - Request AI-powered research assistance from ChatGPT. Ask for information, statistics, or references related to specific subjects or

concepts you want to include in your book.
- Use AI tools to fact-check your writing and ensure accuracy. AI-powered fact-checkers can scan your text and flag potential inaccuracies or provide alternative sources to verify information.

4. Language and Writing Enhancement:
- Seek AI-powered language and writing tools to improve the clarity, coherence, and readability of your book.
- Use AI-driven grammar and spelling checkers to identify and correct errors.
- Employ AI-based style and tone analyzers to ensure consistency and enhance the overall writing quality.

Remember, while AI can be a valuable tool in the writing process, it's essential to maintain your creative vision and critical thinking. AI-generated suggestions should be evaluated and refined according to your unique writing style and goals. Use AI as a supportive resource to enhance your writing process rather than relying on it solely for creative decisions.

By leveraging the capabilities of ChatGPT and AI tools, you can streamline the organization of your book chapters, generate fresh writing ideas, and enhance the overall quality of your manuscript. (Can you tell I used ChatGPT to write this chapter? I'm sure you could! That's how easy it is.)

Secret #11 Celebrate the Little Victories

I'm here at the beach today, and I'm saying let's celebrate your wins. Celebrate the little victories, every little bit. You finish a chapter; you finish a paragraph. You finish celebrating the victory. Give yourself verbal praise, affirmation and pat yourself on the back. You did it. You accomplished it. When you show up in the gym, pat yourself on the back. When you finish a chapter, pat yourself on the back. When you finish a paragraph, Celebrate yourself. Celebrate your win. I'm proud of you. Keep moving forward. That's how the book gets done. Way to go, 52AuthorSecrets.com.

Secret #12 Pre-Launch of Your Book to Build Your Tribe

Here's an idea as an author that you can begin premarketing and promoting your book even before it's live. Do a photo of yourself. Put your QR code and website on the flyer, offer something of value like a free consult, get them on your calendar.

Go to a print shop and print out a poster. You can have it designed on Fiverr.com When you're speaking somewhere or you're networking, somewhere you have something. You can give people something of value, not just a business card.

Truly be different. Truly be authentic. Truly be out of the box so that people remember you. Put your QR code on your poster and your website along with your hashtag.

Anytime you're a guest at an event, have this available on your book table and your swag table. You know what? People are going to remember you. And even for those people who are too tight fisted to spend $25 on a book they leave with you anyway. Be sure and do a selfie with everyone, follow them on social media, be sure your #hastags are on your flyer or poster so you can watch online when they share your selfie, reshare them and comment.

And then you follow up with a daily or weekly dose of inspiration with a video like this one you're watching now, and boom. They're part of your tribe. You invite them to your Facebook group. Every week reward the winner of your hashtag competition with a shout out on social media. You are the brand anytime you and or your face show up your topic is there; your brand is represented. Let people know what you're all about and tell great stories that they'll remember!

Secret #13 Start Marketing Early

Begin the marketing early. Before you write a single word, before you pin a single sentence, before you sit down at the computer, do your research, know who your avatar is, do a deep dive and know what it is you want to accomplish. Do you want to entertain? Do you want to educate? Do you want to inform? Do you want to cause massive action? Do you want to create a movement? Or do you just want to entertain with fiction and give somebody some fiction to read before they go to bed at night? Do your research. Know exactly what it is you want to accomplish. That way, you're always in charge when the book becomes a movie and the movie changes lives with your movement. The best time to start marketing is two years before you launch your book, the second-best time is today! You might be saying, *"Michael I didn't do a good job of marketing when I launched my book and it's been out a while, no problem, do a second edition with updated and expanded content and do a relaunch as if you're launching for the first time!"* Good content NEVER gets old!

Secret #14 Leverage Celebrity Credibility with Implied Endorsements for your Book

As an author You want to leverage celebrity endorsements to grow your book launch. I'm here in downtown Philadelphia. I'm about to go across the street and speak at Temple University on this very topic today.

This is a two-part segment of leveraging the celebrity endorsement. First, the implied endorsement and then getting the direct endorsement. How do I do it? Very simple. I find an author that's launching a book that I want their endorsement. I go to their website, find out their next book signing. I show up at their book signing. Of course, I buy their book and read the book. But then I bring a friend to snap a video and a photo of me with the author. It's an implied endorsement.

Then it gives me the open door. The social door is now open to go in and ask for a direct endorsement on my book.

Secret #15 Get Celebrity Endorsements

Today I'm in Times Square New York City and I'm going to talk to you about how to get a celebrity endorsement for your book. It's very powerful to establish credibility. First off is reach out to your publisher. They can probably help you. And if they can't, and you've got in mind the celebrity author you want to endorse your book, reach out to them directly. In the age of social media, the gatekeeper has been removed. But before you just ask for it, show them some love. Go in, share their social media content with your audience. Better yet, go to one of their book signings as I discussed in the previous secret.

Even if you must wait in line for 5 hours to get a book signed, it'll be well worth it with the endorsement and the credibility of the celebrity author. Now, don't give them your entire book to read. Give them one chapter and a table of contents because they're busy. Respect them and give them three or four examples. Write an endorsement for them where they can choose one or offer some slight edits.

You're more likely to get an endorsement that way. So, you now have it and all because you asked! So go ask and get it. Getting a Celebrity Foreword is the same formula just ask for the foreword instead of the endorsement and yes it helps if you write 2-3 and let them pick one!

Secret #16 Share the Who, What, When, Where, WHY and How of Your Book

This is a KEY to going viral, every week for 5 weeks or better yet, every day for 5 days prior to your book launch go live on social media at the same time and tell the world:

WHO you wrote your book for, (your avatar)
WHAT is the Content of your book?

What happens WHEN others apply the principles of your book to their life?

WHERE your launch party is (that should be an entire Secret in this book but then we'd have 53 author secrets! So consider it a BONUS!)

And most importantly, WHY you wrote your book? (Your WHY should make you cry!)

HOW you wrote your book?

This last one is probably the least important and entertaining but is good info for a press release or long interview where you have time to share about your writing habits and techniques. As your fame and popularity as an author increases more fans will find this insider info interesting about you and love this "director's cut" behind the scenes stuff that didn't make the book, especially if you're a fiction author, fans go crazy over this stuff!

That's right. Every week leading up to your book launch, do a video, go live, share it everywhere, and address who the book is for. Who is your avatar? What is the book about? What is the content that you put in the book? Share testimonials from readers *"what others are saying"* even interview some of your best critics and most critical reviewers, this will REALLY help you get more eyeballs on your pre-sale link when you're willing to take on haters. Remember all press is GOOD press because it means others are talking about you.

The next week, do a video on the why. What is your why with the book? What are you trying to do? Create a movement? Change somebody's mind? Inform? Educate? Entertain?

What is the link? Give me the presell link so they can pre buy it in all its formats and then give us the how, which is how did you write it? People want to know the backstory, so share it everywhere!

Secret #17 Attend Events to Meet People and Sell More Books

How Can You Get More Visible as An Author? It's by attending events, meeting people, and selling more books. Meeting people is where the magic happens. It's how you get booked on podcasts and stages it's how you get discovered and found. It's how you get referred and recommended. Show up, be confident, show interest in others and do some good ole fashioned networking!

Secret #18 Attend Online Events

The second thing to being more visible is going to online events. You can attend online events at home in your pajamas if you like and never have to go to the airport. Zoom has created many millionaires and not just because of the pandemic but many entrepreneurs discovered zoom during the pandemic. Why not monetize those relationships. What groups are you already in that you could talk about your book launching? Take advantage of these relationships and speak up. People want to support you, especially your *"groupies"*.

Secret #19 Host Your Own Events

Are you asking how you can be more visible and sell more books? To make your brand go viral, this WILL give YOU brand ambassadors who pay you to represent your brand. I'll show you how! Framing this context will help you prepare for a proper launch and maximum impact with your book!

We just wrapped up a great women's event with powerful female immigrants **PowerfulFemaleImmigrants.com** from around the world here in Dallas. And here's what I learned.

If you want to be more visible, go to events. That's right. Go to events and meet people because they're going to want to hear what you're doing. They're going to want to buy your book and support your book launch.

Author Yulin Lee is going to Paris next month on vacation. And guess what? She's renting an airbnb and she's hosting a mastermind with eight women. And guess what? They're becoming brand evangelists for her because they're a part of her book launch and her brand. Her book, **Unleashed: Tapping into Your Feminine Instinct to Create Financial Independence** will be seen all over Europe and beyond! Now, that's how you become visible!

Host Online Events with reminders that either you're the speaker or you invite experts to interview on your show and they'll get an email reminder when the time's coming. If they've RSVP, add your Buy Now book link to your email signature so that every time somebody gets an email from you, they know you're the best-selling author of a book called XYZ, and they can click and go buy it or leave you a review. Do a text marketing campaign where you capture text messages and remind them about your weekly online event.

Secret # 21 Be Memorable When Launching Your Book

You want to stick in people's memories so that they think of you when they need to hire a speaker, when they need to interview somebody for their media show or podcast. How do you stick in their head and remain top of mind? Will you do a video about your book?

For example, here's my first book, the Single Dad's Survival Guide. Every Father's Day, I do a bunch of media interviews around this book. I really believe in video. I believe you could go live at the same time every day of the week where you share behind the scenes about your book. You could actually do video chapters around each chapter of your book doing a deep dive and explaining the behind-the-scenes reasons you wrote that chapter.

You could bring on guests that you talk about in the book and that you refer to in the book as illustrations and stories and principles around your book. You can get on local news media and do PR around that. I'll talk more about that in a future video. And finally, you can tie your book to a nonprofit and donate a portion of the proceeds from the sale of your book to support that nonprofit more soon with. The main thing is to be memorable and stick in people's memories, so they think about. The best way to be memorable is to be a master storyteller. The reason storytelling did not get its own chapter is so much of these secrets are powered by great storytelling. Have a repertoire of personal stories, business stories, call to action stories, money making stories, motivational stories, come to Jesus stories ready to tell at a moment's notice. Have the 30 second, 3-minute, and the 30-minute version ready to go. Some day you might get asked to fill in for someone's online television show or telethon and need to cover 30 hours. Be prepared to tell epic stories by mastering the art of being a master storyteller right now.

Begin to practice the art of being a master storyteller now on friends and family without them even knowing it. They will start to lean in, listen and like you even more because of how you make them feel!

Secret #22 The Power of the Non-Profit

I've been preaching the power of the non-profit for decades. For most authors I don't advocate starting your own non-profit, it's too much work. Partner with a non-profit that aligns with your values that you feel good promoting, donating to and bragging about. This goes a long way to in furthering your brand as someone who cares about causes. You can even designate a portion of your proceeds from your royalties to your favorite non-profit. Thirty percent of the revenue of Beyond Publishing goes to rescue girls from human trafficking at 1040Impact.org

Secret #23 Practice Your Pitch- Nail the Sound Bite

We're talking today about practice your pitch. And we're talking about your book pitch. If you're an author, you want to practice your pitch. This is also called the "elevator pitch" what you'd say to someone if you only had 10-20 seconds on an elevator. You want to nail the sound bite of who your book is for. Give us the hook. And practice. Practice, practice, practice. Practice with your family and friends. Practice till you get the hole in one. You want to practice your pitch. Who's your book for? Why did you write it? What are the takeaways? It's really about the information you'll put on the back of the book. Who is it for? And one of the best hooks is sharing testimonials. Practice those testimonials. Go live once a week. Share behind the scenes why you wrote the book, who it's for, who it's going to help? And keep sharing those testimonials. Does your pitch: 1) Grab Attention? 2) Create Curiosity? 3) Tell A Story? 4) Tell us Who You are? 5) How you change lives? 6) Have a call to Action - How do People Find You and Get on Your Calendar? It's great to finish your elevator pitch with, *"give me your card or phone number so I can follow up with you and we can collaborate more."*

Secret #24 Getting Comfortable with Video to Promote Your Book

Why is marketing with video so important? It's how you sell more books. And what I want to deal with today is I want to deal with confidence. You know, before you can do anything with confidence, it takes practice. It just means picking up your phone going live, hitting that red record button. Because the first time you rode a bike, you didn't do it perfectly.

You probably fell off the first time you tried to drive a car. Maybe you wrecked it like I did. It took practice. It takes a while to get used to it and to get the confidence. And the best way to sell your book is to get confident. Tell me why you wrote your book. Who's it for? Who do you want to read your book? Tell us the best story of someone's experience from reading your book.

Secret #25 Consistency Can Produce Effective Results

Going live every week or every day on your social media, getting out there with video, getting your presence, connecting with your tribe, building a tribe, adding value to your tribe, and being consistent. I'm doing a consistent 52 author video each week for 52 weeks. 52 Author Secrets. And within that, I've embedded these six videos on video marketing for your book as an author. And so be consistent like that. Come up with a theme that serves your brand. Come up with a theme that's going to bring leads and generate not just book readers, but members to your website. Members of your tribe that are going live.

To become raving fans that are going to want to share not only your book launch, but you're behind the scenes. Your book signings, your Amazon bestsellers, your Amazon reviews, everything about your book launch entails. That's called creating a family. People want to belong in your family, so get out there and create that!

Secret #26 The Power of Clarity in Your Video Marketing

Clarity is the key that will give you everything you want when pre-launching your book. Watch the video to find out how! Framing this context will help you prepare for a proper launch and maximum impact with your book! Michael D. Butler here on 52AuthorSecrets.com and CEO of Beyond Publishing. Today's, Author Tip is using video and using it with clarity. We talked about using video confidently, using video consistency consistently. Today I'm talking about be very clear with your message and what you want people to do. So, for example, when you shoot your video, tell them at the end of the video, go follow me on social media and then include the link so they can follow you. Tell them exactly what you want them to do. Go to Amazon, download my eBook, read through it, and then leave a five-star review. Be very clear and ask them what you want them to do. So, what I want you to do right now is I want you to click the link and go watch all 52 of my Author Tips. You'll be better prepared to write a best seller and to go bestseller before you launch, and to engage a tribe of Raving fans. Thank you very much.

Secret #27 Social Media Secrets in 60 Second Videos

Do you want to know how to use video to blow up your book launch in brand? I'm going to show you in the next 60 seconds. You know, two of my sons are trained culinary specialists, and they said, dad, it's all about the preparation and the presentation because there's only four food groups. So, what I want you to do, you're already a master at producing content.

See how I did it before writing this book at www.52AuthorSecrets. com I have literally produced 52 videos on YouTube covering each of these topics you are reading now in a video in various major cities of the world. Go ahead and subscribe and leave a comment and let me know you found me on **Book Idea to Bestseller in 30 Days**. and tell me what you're writing now so I can go comment and follow you!

You wrote a book. So now I want you to strategically share it on the internet. Put those breadcrumbs out there, intrigue, engage, ask questions. Create a hook. Create anticipation.

Let your readers smell it and feel it. Give us a peek behind the scenes. Why you wrote it. What's in it for them? How can they benefit? Share testimonials and stories to further increase engagement and impressions.

Reshare those testimonials and those endorsements and those five-star reviews. Share it. Drive it to your coaching program. You know what? Nobody gets super wealthy off their book.

But if you treat the content strategically, consistently, confidently, you're going to build a huge brand. Keep it up- I'm proud of you and the world is watching!

"This is the pebble that creates the ripple that becomes the movement!"
Michael D. Butler

Two of my sons are trained culinary specialists, and they said, *"dad, it's all about the preparation and the presentation because there's only four food groups."* So, what I want you to do is keep sharing, engaging and adding value to your followers with thoughtful video content on a consistent basis for the next three years. *"Three years are you kidding me?"* I'm absolutely serious! If you were starting a traditional brick and mortar business you'd work full time for five years and 90% of the time, still be failing and in the red. You don't expect to make a profit your first five years in a traditional business so how can you expect to be successful as an author after only two interviews and three social media posts? You need to come at this with realistic expectations. Remember Jack Canfield and Mark Victor Hansen did 600 radio interviews that first year they launched Chicken Soup for the Soul. They didn't go on to sell half a billion books because they were sipping margaritas on the beach every day, they worked hard and continued to work hard for years before it paid off. One you're that determined to never give ups, keep talking, keep making video, keep adding value to your audience then your success will be closer than you think!

Secret #28 It's All About Packaging – Cover Design

Is your book properly packaged? I'm talking about book covers, and I'm talking about the power of the package to get somebody to buy your book. First, you got to get them to pick it up. And the way to get them to read the back of the book is to intrigue them with the COVID Did you know cereal companies spend more on the package than they do the content of the box?

That's right. It's all about the branding. Ladies, would you rather get a gift delivered in a brown paper bag or a blue tiffany box? It's all about the packaging. Package your content properly so that the book cover creates intrigue and readers ask questions.

We're talking about the book title and the subtitle and the visual aesthetics to get people to turn to the back cover and see if your book is right for them. So properly package with your book cover and begin to presell your book with your cover before your content is even complete.

Recently one of our authors from North Carolina called me, David, a business coach was a little stressed out. I asked David why he was anxious, and he said, "I've got a major TV interview in the morning and my books not done yet." I said, "no problem, go to the print shop, I'll email you the cover, you can faux scotch tape it up wrap another book from your library, hold up "your book" as if it's done, do the interview, send people to your website and pretend as if it's available." He did exactly that, pre-sold 39 books from his website, picked up two coaching clients, collected the data on those 39 people who went to his site and shipped them their books within two weeks. Some people see challenges, others see opportunity.

Attending a business conference in Vegas recently an Author named Alan from Michigan hired me to publish his book to create credibility. Alan is Michigan's largest door and window manufacturer and I learned Alan was speaking on the state at an event in Maui the next week for another author and speaker that I know and respect named Bob Harrison at his Increase event. I said, "Alan, I'll fly to Maui next week and help you pre-sell your books" and you'll have an instant bestseller. And that's exactly what happened my company, Beyond Publishing created a book cover for him in a few days, we got it up online for pre-sell with zero content inside. We go number one in Maui when he's speaking, get a ton of pre-orders, three months later when we're done with the manuscript, we help him launch **My Jewish Secret** his bestselling book in the personal finance and wealth categories. We've since gone on to launch another of his great books called **Trading Options** and these are just three more great examples that you can execute too when you know who your avatar is, are clear on what action you want them to take you don't have to wait for the content to be complete you can literally pre-sell your book before it's even done!

Secret #29 The Power of Controversy to Sell More Books

Do you want to create buzz around your book, around your brand and book sales, where there's five C's that sell books, cover design, conversation, content, and context? And then there's my favorite controversy. That's right, creating some good old-fashioned controversy around your brand. When you look at iconic billion-dollar brands, personal brands, in the music industry and other literary industries, you're going to find that they all started with controversy. Not controversy all the time. That would get a little much, but maybe 20% of the time on your social media and on your press releases, you take the other side's point of view. If you're doing fiction or nonfiction, it can't hurt. It will only help and enhance your brand, because it's going to get other people talking about you. All PR is good PR if people are talking about you right?

Secret #30 Use Targeted Networking Events to Blow Up Your Book

One of the best ways to grow your business is to attend live events. I talked about this in Secret #17-#19 This time I want to drill down a little further. Attend at least six to eight live events per year and twelve to twenty-four virtual events per year. I'm saying that's the best way to grow is to get out of your house and network and make things happen. Today I'm here at eWomen Network in Dallas, Texas today; this is a global organization. And my reach and my target market are women.

Women over 40. And so that's why I come to women's events. I sponsor women's events. Women's events are our bread and butter.

In fact, I like to say, **"I love women. I love women's events. And I love sponsoring women's events."**

Showing up and saying this the last 3 year has produced hundreds of thousands of dollars for our publishing business! The best way to grow your business, to grow your book launch, and to grow awareness about your brand, is to get out and network at events like this one on-one meeting new people, getting to know them, asking questions and seeing how you can be a joint venture partner. Start connecting and asking questions like, *"who is a good referral for you?"* And see what happens!

Secret #31 Selling More Books by Attending Book Shows

To sell more books you must go where the buyers are. We go to all the global book shows abroad and in the USA every year. We've been to Jerusalem, Bogota Colombia. Guadalajara, Mexico, Frankfurt, Germany. Bologna, Italy and many others.

And you know what? There's dozens and dozens, if not hundreds of book shows in the USA where you can go promote your book, meet bookstore owners, meet distributors, meet people that want to have you speak on their stage. Here's a list of some of the global and USA based book shows. Get yourself booked out for 2023. I was recently in Korea, Vietnam, and Thailand promoting books for our authors. You could be there. Learn more, get yourself booked, and let's sell more of your books!

Secret #32 Get Your Book into Bookstores

Have you wanted to get your book into bookstores? The two things you need to get your book into bookstores. Number one, and check with your publisher on this, your book needs to be enabled for distribution. And number two, returns need to be enabled so that the bookstore doesn't have financial liability if somebody returns the book.

Those are the two things you need, and your publisher can let you know. Now, 90% of the time, if you're self-published, it's hard, almost impossible, to get into bookstores and libraries. But if you got those two things enabled, you can get into bookstores and libraries. If you want to do a deep dive on how to get into more bookstores, just Google my name, **"Michael D. Butler and bookstores"** on YouTube. Watch those four videos that I did with Claude Collins and de de Cox and you're going to love them. You're going to learn so much about getting into bookstores, and you can get into bookstores right away.

Secret #33 Use Advance Reader Copies to Sell More Books

Advance reader copies, also known as galley copies, are pre-launch books (maybe with a few unedited pages in it) to get into the hands of influencers you're seeking an early endorsement from. An ARC is a pre-published book that you send out in advance to get a copy into the hands of influencers, book bloggers and people in the media who you want them to interview you or say something nice about your book or have you on their podcast.

And you literally just send out a copy of your book that is a table of contents and a few chapters and the official book cover, but it's not complete yet. And you send them this book to a short list of 25, 50, maybe 100 people on the list that you're wanting them to give you a good review about your book. So, an advanced reader copy can be very beneficial. And you spend a year or two writing your book. Why not spend six months premarketing your book, getting endorsements from the advanced reader copies, and getting media interviews. Now go hit a home run with advanced reader copies. Ask your publisher they may have an ARC program you can leverage for your book launch.

Secret #34 Get Yourself into the News Media with Press Releases

I've been teaching authors how to get their book, business, and brand into the local, regional, and National news media for years. The first thing you need to get into the media on any level is a unique story and a compelling hook.

Do you want to get your book into the news media? Do you want to get yourself on TV and into the media talking about your book and your message? This is the time when producers, editors, and media companies are looking for people with content. And one of the best ways to get your book out there is to ask yourself the question, what is the media hook? What is the hook that the media is looking for? So, if you wrote a book on overcoming grief, now is a perfect time to target the media because you know what?

During the holidays, a lot of people are depressed. Suicides are at an all-time high because of family issues, because of the holidays, people get depressed. And so, ask yourself, what is the hook? Even if you wrote a fiction book, what is the hook? What is the talking point around getting you on the news and talking about your book? So, you can also create news by sponsoring an event, by donating books to Little League, donating books to Literacy Foundation, to Junior Achievement, to Scouts, to Girl Scouts, to Boy Scouts. There are all kinds of things you can do in your community that become newsworthy.

Learn how to write a press release, how to draft a compelling headline to hook the media, and how to create your own news. People are the new media, so it's important to be thinking ahead 30, 60, 90 days ahead. What are they going to want on their show on National Grief Awareness Month? Alzheimer's Awareness Month. Diabetes Prevention Month.

Be thinking about be looking ahead and saying, okay, you did a book on wellness. That's great. Well, what are the things that producers are going to want on their show with the timeslots they have to fill in the coming weeks and months?

Maybe it's childhood diabetes month? Maybe it's fertility awareness week? Maybe it's remarriage and finding love again after 60? How do you find love? How do you fall back in love? How does your marriage survive infidelity? How do you blend a family? How do you retire early? How do you resurrect your finances in a recession?

All these things' people are asking, and these are the solutions your producers and show hosts are looking to fill with interviews. How do you save money through the winter when utility bills are high? What do you do when unemployment is high? How do you make yourself marketable to get hired? Ask yourself, what problem does my book solve? What is my message around my book? What are the talking points in my book that help people get a competitive edge? You've got to realize the interview is about the listener. It's about the audience. It's not at all about you as the speaker. So, you don't want to come in selling your book, but you want to come in with the solutions.

"In chapter three, I give a ten-point checklist to XYZ." You want to share that with them and provide value. Provide value. Provide value. And guess what? You're going to get booked again and again and again. Congratulations How to Get Your Book, Business and Brand into the Local, Regional and National News Media

Secret #35 Use Press Releases for SEO and Backlinks to Your Website

So, there's two reasons to get into the news: 1) Social proof that you're making an impact with your message that you screenshot and reshare on social media and 2) For the valuable backlinks and SEO it gives you on your website.

"A good PR story is infinitely more effective than a front-page ad." **Sir Richard Branson**

Do you want your book launch in the news media? Let me tell you the best way. It's Michael Butler here. Beyond Publishing published 789 books in the last five years, and many of those clients, we've gotten into the news media with a nationally syndicated press release that we write, a clever headline and summary keyword rich meta description, meta tags, SEO enabled that's optimized search engine optimized. That's going to be a powerful backlink to your website. And we're going to get dozens and dozens, sometimes hundreds of media websites to link to that and reshare that story about your book launch.

So, we share the meat and potatoes of your book launch, what your book is about, who you wrote your book for, what you want the book to do, if you're available for media interviews and for speaking on stages and what your book is going to do for the world. So, it's very exciting. We put that press release out one to two weeks before your book is launched, but after your presale link has gone live. And what this does, it creates media buzz. It gets you picked up on ABC, NBC, CBS, Fox News. It gives you a valuable SEO backlink, lots of valuable SEO backlinks to your websites. It gives you social proof. It gives you all the social proof. We give you the report of all the media sites that have picked this story up about you and about your book launch. And the other thing, you take the content that we write for the press release, and you put it on your website a good week before the press release goes live. And therefore, your content becomes the cornerstone content of the media because everybody's linking back to you.

It drives book sales. It gets you media attention. You use the screenshots of the media pickups for social proof of the fact that your books launched, and that people are talking about your book and the social proof as seen on Fox, ABC, NBC, CBS. We do all this for you because it drives traffic to your brand and to your Buy Now link. So, if you want more media interviews, you've got to get to the media the way that they want to be reached, and that is through press releases. Listen, the media journalists are subscribing to the newswires that we syndicate out to base on the keywords. Congratulations you on your book launch. Take advantage of it. Don't squander this opportunity. Launch it properly with the press release a cleverly written press release and get ready to leverage everything that produces for you.

Secret #36 Use Public Speaking to Grow Your Book Business and Brand

Using Speaking to grow your book, your business, and your brand. Today I talk about how to get more speaking gigs. Zig Ziggler said he gave a thousand free speaking gigs before he ever got paid for a speech. In the internet age I think you're learning curve as a new speaker can be much shorter. But if you're willing to give 100 free speeches you're well on your way to mastering the art of public speaking to sell more books.

I just got through speaking here at Temple University about that very concept to a room full of 50 people. And you know what? There are free speaking gigs everywhere where you can promote your book, sell your book, and get people to sign up for your membership website, your online community, your weekly email. And it's all about relationship. You want to provide value, provide free content.

Like I did up here. I had everybody text me the word book to my cell phone at 918-955-3227 so I could give them access to my video course **CredibilityBook.LIVE** to help them finish their book. Since you've read this far into **BOOK IDEA TO BESTSELLER** you can have access to it to, use promo code: **BEYOND** to get free access and jump on my calendar once you've completed it so we can talk about your book!

Did you know you can speak for free at Rotary Clubs all over America? There are hundreds of organizations like this that you can speak at across the country and the world!

Speaking is one of the best ways to grow your business and your brand and sell more books. Speak at local civic groups, toastmasters, church groups everywhere the doors are open. Rotary club. Optimus club, Junior Achievement, do your research to see which groups align more closely to your values. I show you how to get into those groups, how to get on their list, their speaker list, and you get to sell books there, and you get to make money there, and you get to drive traffic there and speaking at local groups.

In my bestselling book ***FINDING THE SPEAKER'S EDGE - Turning Your Part-Time Passion into Your Full-Time Professional Speaking Career on Stage and Online***

has helped hundreds of people get out there and start speaking and start speaking for pay. I show how you can carve out a nice niche in the global speaking industry that is growing from its current level of $8 billion a year industry to a $100 billion dollar a year industry by 2030!

Secret #37 Get Your Audio Book Selling to the World on Audible, ACX and iTunes

Do you listen to audiobooks? I listen to a ton of audiobooks, about five or six a week. And I love audiobooks because I'm always on the go. Right now, I'm training for my next marathon and I'm always at the gym or in my car, and I'm always listening to audiobooks. And one way I do it is I crank it up 2x speed. If you don't have your book out as an author in audible format in audiobook, you are missing out because audio increase is going up 200% per year. You want to read it in your own voice. You don't want to hire somebody to read it. If you do hire somebody to read it, talk to me, because we've got some opportunities for you. If you're one of our authors. We can help you get your audiobook out to the world. And if you just need help getting your audiobook out to the world, reach out to me. As an author you must get your audio book out for maximum exposure and distribution of your book!

Secret #38 Get on More Podcasts as an Author and Speaker

Media has changed and traditional media, while still important is losing eyeballs year over year. New Media like podcasts, social media and digital platforms offer authors, speakers, and experts the opportunity to reach a wider audience. Let's face it, if you're not talking, no one is buying and the best way to sell books and get people to your website is to get on those podcasts and be a master storyteller! A great free resource to get on more podcasts is The Author Community on Facebook at TheAuthorCommunity.com. Check them out. If you're a Beyond Publishing author we give you your first media interview for free and even coach you on your talking points, what to say and what questions to have the host ask you.

Secret #39 Hire AI and ChatGPT to be your CMO

How can an author use artificial intelligence to grow their business, their book, their brand, get more speaking gigs, get on more stages? Hey, listen. Artificial Intelligence and Chat GPT. They're here to stay. They're not going anywhere. And you can either ignore it and go in your cave, or you can participate and benefit. Our authors use ChatGPT to get ideas on potential titles and subtitles, organizing their Table of Contents, writing press releases and marketing content not to mention do the preliminary research on who to write the book for and help on filling in some content with creative stories and subplots, yes ChatGPT can do all of that and more, give it a try and see what else you can come up with!

You're going to be epic.

Secret #40 Get Your Books into Libraries in the USA and Globally

Hi, authors. Do you want to get your book into libraries? Did you know libraries are the number one buyers of books globally? That's right. Libraries love books. And they don't just buy one or two books. They buy dozens of books at a time. If you sell your books to the library in Santa Monica, California, they're not just going to buy one or two books, they're going to buy 38 books. And particularly, they love hardcover books. But it's very important that your book have a library of congress control number and that you publish or mail in hard copies of your books to the library of Congress in Washington, DC. To make that happen. There are some other things you can do to make that happen. If you want to jump on my calendar, jump on my calendar link right there and watch all the videos. At 52 authorsecrets.com, I'm your host, Michael D. Butler. At 50, twoauthorsecrets.com, let's get you in the libraries and selling around the world. You four. Authors Do This to Get Your Books into Libraries in the USA and Globally.

Secret #41 Get into Little Libraries as Well

How little do we know about the effectiveness of the free libraries based around the USA? Despite their small size design, the impact is everlasting. Find out how you can benefit from these little libraries. WATCH NOW #16 of 52 Watch the video to find out how! Framing this context will help you prepare for a proper launch and maximum impact with your book!

Today's secret is lending your book to a library. That's right, this little free library or across America, across the world. If you really want to promote and market your book, you need a marketing budget. One of the best ways to do it is getting your book out into these free libraries. People that love to read will pass your book around, leave reviews on Amazon and everywhere. That's one way to be omniscient, to be everywhere. Get your book out there. And this is one great way to do it. Yes, it's going to cost you a little bit, but it's going to pay rich dividends in the long run. Make it happen littlefreelibrary.org.

Secret #42 Become a Promoter

Hi, authors. Are you a little depressed about your book sales and your book's not really moving? Let me ask you a question. When was the last time you talked about your book from stage? When was the last time you talked about your book on a podcast or held up your book?

I don't think anyone is born a promoter, it's something we all must learn if we want to be successful in our book business.

Exit Rich by my friends Sharon Lecter and Michelle Seiler-Tucker, is just that, it's a book that they've promoted the heck out of. Every time I share the stage with Sharon Lecter, New

York Times bestselling author, and I've shared the stage with her many times. She talks about her next five books. She's holding up several books. She's giving away books to the audience. And she's signing up people for her mastermind. To be successful in this business you must be a shameless self-promoter. I can remember during Covid she spent a lot of time on the social media app Clubhouse, and she added a ton of value to everyone in the room and she'd always share stories from one of her books and tie people into an online event she was hosting or invite them to her ranch for a platinum mastermind. Sharon is the author of the *Rich Dad Poor Dad* series I talk about in the first half of this book that has sold over 30 million copies. Sharon is the consummate promoter. She has been very successful and even though she could retire, she chooses to keep speaking and keep adding value to people and continues to; coach, speak and write books!

My question for you as an author, when was the last time you went live and talked about your book? When was the last time you posted on social media about your book? When was the last time you shared from stage about your book? Perhaps your book has not come out yet, that's even more reason to be talking about what's coming. Feature your book cover, launch your podcast around your book topic, promote the upcoming launch. Share the pre-order link so people can pre-buy your book. All of this adds up to big things for you both now and in

the future. You are planting seeds that will come back and take care of you in your old age!

If you're an author and you're depressed with book sales, look in the mirror, and start promoting. Become a promoter. *"Well, I'm a humble person,"* you say? Now's not the time to be humble. You just wrote a book.

"Timid salespeople have skinny children."
Zig Ziglar

Are you wanting to have the most impact with your book as an author during your book launch and reintroducing your book? You know, on this show, 52 authorsecrets.com and my new book launching later this year here at 52 Author Secrets, we've published over 740 books in the last six years. I'm your host, Michael D. Butler. And sometimes looking at digital marketing and social media, we forget to look at traditional marketing things that you can do to grow your business.

Secret #43 Print Business Cards, bookmarkers print flyers and announcements that you post at coffee shops. Do gifts and free offers to promote with. Do a hashtag scavenger hunt. That's where you put a hashtag that you're using to promote your book on everything. It's got your book title and your book cover. Let the world know you are launching around the globe and beyond! Elon Musk sent a Tesla to space for the sheer marketing value and to say, *"I can do that!"* Where have you planted your book lately? Yes, even in the digital age do not underestimate the good ole fashioned value of print marketing!

Secret #44 Virtual Book Tours have people hold up copies of your book around the globe as they take pictures and share pictures with them holding up your book and your hashtag. And then they get a gift. Maybe you give them a free audiobook or maybe you send them something in the mail. Mail out announcement cards. Print up announcement cards and mail those out to friends and family. Start with friends and family their always eager to help but also grab total strangers at the airport and finally turn to Fiverr.com to get some added help on this.

Secret #45 Create a Mascot

Now this secret is definitely out of the box and fun. When I was in the ministry, I spent some years as a Children's Pastor and we had some full sized costumes for my team to do workshops and presentations for the kids in the classroom and in the auditorium. We had full sized clowns, gorillas, dinosaurs, Biblical characters, you name it we had it.

Who said you had to stop having fun after you become an adult? Adopting a mascot is cool and fun and makes you memorable. Even if you're not writing children's book think about what mascot you could create to help you promote your book? Sports teams have mascots, Fortune 500 companies have mascots, why not create a mascot for your book launch? If you write about money create a money centric mascot. If you write about relationships do giant hearts, if you write about technology and AI, use your imagination!

Secret #46 Text Message Campaigns Did you know text messages are opened 95% of the time compared to email, which only has about 20% or less opt in rate and open rate. So do text marketing. Be consistent, add value, educate, ask questions, mix it up with a variety of content and your fans will be loving you and expecting more!

Secret #47 Buy a Pop-Up Banner like a step and repeat or a spring-loaded pop-up banner from a sign shop that you can bring with you when you're speaking or doing a book signing at a library or a bookstore. And be sure to take lots of photos, lots of photos everywhere you're out promoting your book and getting book signings done. Have copies of your book in the trunk of your car and be sure and sign those books. And get pictures with people that are reviewing your book and sharing your book. You want to make it go viral?

Secret #48 Get a Story in Your Local Newspaper. Local is the new global. To be a national rock star, start local! Visit ChatGPT and ask her to help you write a press release for your local paper, you'll be surprised how quick and easy that is. Attach a photo, find out who covers local authors at the local paper and you're in! Then you can repurpose that story to get you into the regional, statewide and national news!

Secret #49 Launch an Online Show around your topic. Spend each week going deep into each chapter of your book at the same time on that online show.

Here's a big one. Be a guest on other people's podcasts. I show you how to do this on. 52AuthorSecrets.com Learn how to ask questions. Ask lots of questions and see where it takes you!

Start conversations. Start conversations in the elevator. Start conversations in the line at the grocery store. And everywhere people congregate, let them know you're an author and you've got a book that solves relationships problems, that solves money problems, that solves health and nutrition and wellness and weight loss problems. Whatever problem your book solves, then go online to those groups that are talking about those topics.

And don't just come in there selling but introduce yourself by asking questions. Asking questions. And then people, once they learn who you are, they'll want to check out what you have. And the other thing you can do is lots of swag. Buy T shirts.

Secret #50 Buy Some Swag to Promote Your Book

Nothing says your serious about your book and your message like printing some swag. Hats, shirts, coffee mugs, book markers, the more swag the better. Think about what your reader likes and stock that. Ink pens, golf paraphernalia, etc.… By being seen everywhere over time as you ask your new customers, "how did you hear about us." You'll start seeing a trend and be able to track how effective you're advertising and marketing dollars are.

Secret #51 Wrap Your Vehicle

If you drive a lot like I do it makes sense to wrap your vehicle with your brand and your website so thousands of people can see you each week. Make it colorful and simple, not too busy, clear call to action and a QR code with your website on each side of your vehicle left, right and back. People can scan your QR code and go straight to your website to opt in for a free chapter of your book while they are sitting at a red light. Once in your data base you can drip market to them with weekly emails about your upcoming book launch events, book signings and connect them with your other social media.

Secret #52 Digital Marketing Including Free Offers on Your Website

Emails, email signature, text campaigns, go live.

Bonus Secret #53: BOOK LAUNCH PARTY CHECKLIST

Authors have you ever asked the question, where can I find a complete, comprehensive book launch checklist? You're about ready to launch your fiction or non-fiction book and you asked, is there a checklist anywhere where I can make sense of all the things that I need to do to launch my book properly at a live event, online event, or a hybrid in-person and online even?

Thanks to Charla Anderson, best-selling author of *Candy Bar Hugs,* and *Split-Second Transformations* Charla was asking us in our author Mastermind, Is there a checklist? I said, I'll create one. So, this is for you the bonus chapter in Book Idea to Bestseller. You've seen me all over the media promoting this book from Detroit, San Antonio, and Colorado, and everywhere on television in the USA and Beyond. This is the book to help get your Book Idea to Best Seller in 30 days.

In just 6 years we've published over 791 titles in the last six years with authors in 64 nations and here's what we've learned:

1) Define your goals and your audience
2) Select a venue
3) Select the date and the time
4) Create an event page on social media like Facebook and Eventbrite, so you can gather people's data and collect their information, and they can get pop up reminders for them that they're going to see it as it approaches. You want

to do this at least 30 to 45 days out, if not more, to keep it growing, keep your RSVP list growing, and then every day

5) Go there and post something that's going on around the book promotion

6) Design some eye-catching memes and promotional materials that you can tweet out, you can share on social media

7) Send out some save-the-date announcements just like you would a wedding invitation or graduation in the mail

8) Do a pre-order campaign. You want to create that with your publisher, the live pre-order link so that your hardback, your paperback, and e-book are all available for presale. This will help juice the Google and Amazon algorithms to make you a best-selling author

9) Work with your publisher to be sure you hit Bestseller status on Amazon

10) Put these pre-sell links in all of your correspondence, your emails, and your event on social media so people can pre-buy the book

11) Do as many interviews on podcasts and media outlets as possible, leading up to your book launch. The more you speak, the more books you sale

12) Put out a press release

13) Invite local media to your Book Launch Party - Reach out to the local media, invite them to come, send personalized invitations to local media, book bloggers, and literary influencers

14) Have an itinerary for your event and what's going to happen in each five-minute segment of that event.

15) Build a book signing around the event

16) Have pop up banners that promote you and your book (this is great for photographs and book signing tables too

17) Have enough copies of your books on hand to sell, hand out, and give away as gifts

18) Do some door prizes and swag bags for your attendees

19) Invite a nonprofit organization of your choice to attend. Maybe you have a nonprofit or somebody you want to include that runs a nonprofit, bring them to the event, have them share for five minutes, let them have a little table or booth and to promote the why of your book. For example, we're passionate about 1040impact.org, the non-profit I founded and the work they do to rescue kids from human trafficking. We care for 400+ girls in four safe houses ages 6-17 whom we've rescued and feed them and our full-time staff of 25 more than 50,000 meals a month. These girls are being prepared for success in life through our school and career placement programs

20) Livestream on social media, so people all around the world can watch and participate
Meet with your venue and technical support staff the day before your event so everything goes smoothly

21) I recommend hiring an event planner, a photographer, a videographer just to make sure everything goes off without a hitch

22) Print marketing collateral to capture all those magic moments and follow up with putting together videos, sizzle reels, and photographs of the events that are going to live online forever

23) Do another press release after you have a successful event of you doing the book signing, speaking and everything, and having your sponsors there

24) Have some local business partners sponsor your book launch event. particularly if it's at a brick-and-mortar venue. If it's at a winery, or a restaurant, or a bookstore, or a church, let them be a sponsor. List them on your advertising and event fliers and online promotions. Let them write a check to be a sponsor. Let them donate free food or drinks. You'd be surprised if you just start asking local businesses what they're willing to do for a mention.

25) Ask businesses, entrepreneurs and other authors donate to your swag bags. Once you have the date selected and your flyers printed and you let them know people are coming, most business owners will want to donate something to your gift bag. They'll want to donate something from their or their operations

   If it's a spa, perhaps it's a restaurant or whoever it might be, they're going to want to include some coupons to get traffic into their businesses. Maybe they're a business in that same downtown area or next door, they can especially benefit

26) Invite Celebrities - The other thing you want to do, apart from local partnerships, is you want to invite celebrities.

Now, Charla is having her book launch in Fort Worth, and there's a lot of cowboys and ropers and bull riders and steer wrestlers that are in the rodeo world, they're in the cowboy world, that could come out and speak or make an appearance or do a roping demonstration or whatever you want, inviting celebrities, having celebrities at your event is huge to get more people there

27) Get branded with a celebrity - Because everybody's going to want pictures with the celebrity, be sure you get pictures with your book with the celebrity and your attendees is required. They're on the red carpet in front of your banner, but they're also always holding your book. So, it's good for your branding. You can even charge $20 per photo and half goes to your non-profit of choice and half goes help cover the cost of your event. Everybody gets a picture with the celebrity, but they're holding your book for the branding

And so Local Business Partnerships invite celebrities, author book giveaways. You're going to have plenty of paperbacks and hard coverage there. We did a launch recently at McMinnville, Oregon, at the Air and Space Museum. And this young girl, 21, wrote a great best-selling fiction work called Dustin' Blood, a supernatural fiction. And she out of books. In fact, she sold $4,000 worth of books. She wished she had more books. It was a big success

28) Offer your coaching program, upsell promotions into your Mastermind or whatever you got going on next. Maybe

it's an online webinar. You've invited the media. You send formal invitations out to local media, TV, radio, newspapers, and online functions. Follow up with a press kit, personal pitches. I mentioned having your events support staff, that's very important even if they're volunteer, do a run through the day before an event rehearsal so you're not missing anything

Always plan for contingencies and say something goes wrong. You always have a backup plan if the power goes out or something, the sound system doesn't work properly. Event registration and checklist is huge. Your volunteers and your event coordinator can help you with this. I recommend Eventbrite because you're going to get everybody's email address even if it's a pre-event, which you can charge for this. You can charge $5, $10, $20, or whatever. You charge a certain amount; they get a book and a gift bag. So, talk to your local business owners in the area about Swag bags. Talk to your other author friends. Talk to other authors at Beyond Publishing about them donating their book into your Swag bag. Decorate. You don't have to spin an arm and a leg on this, but just a little color, a little flare around your branding. I know, Charlotte, she's turquoise, just like Beyond Publishing logo, she's that color. You'll see her color, her branded color. She's like, This color right here on Powerful Female Immigrants. That's her brand colors. If you're not going to speak, if you're not comfortable as the author speaking at this event, have a designated speaker there with you or have somebody like me interview about why you wrote the book and what's on the inside.

Send thank you notes to the celebrity speakers, local businesses, and the media and participants who helped you. By incorporating all these elements, you can have a very successful book launch. The main thing about it is to follow up. You've created this family now, this tribe of people, so why not start a Facebook group called Split Second Transformations, selling author Charla Anderson. You've got your candy bar hugs, followers in there, and you've got your rating fans around Split Second Transformations. Now they're saying, when's your next book coming out. So be consistent, be bold, be courageous, have fun. You're throwing a party. So, think about a party, a Thanksgiving party, a happy party to bring people together and celebrate. And it's also a chance for you to say thank you to all your friends who have helped you get to where you are. Charla runs a great podcast, and what you might want to do is invite every podcast guest you've ever had, go on their podcast to promote your book, and the list goes on and on.

Have a successful book launch. Be sure and tag me when you're launching your next book. All these books that I've done have had successful book launch parties, both virtual and in-person. I got a lot more books, but these are the main four that I talk about, is have fun, celebrate.

Throwback pictures When social media sites say, hey, a year

ago you were doing this, or Last month you were doing this, share it again. Say, Here's a Thursday throwback to my book launch party. I'll give you a free $500 value book consultant in 15 minutes. Ask me any question about your book. bookstores, libraries, everywhere. Ask me a question about your book. Jump on my calendar link right now and I'll give you some honest feedback. I'm not afraid to tell you if your baby looks ugly. I'll see you at your next book launch.

Congratulations.

Michael D. Butler

52AuthorSecrets.com

Do have a passion to get paid for speaking on stage?

Know a dad going through a divorce?

This is the #1 resource for Single Dads-grab it now!

Discover DATING, LOVE and ROMANCE all over again

Learn How to Write Your Book in 1 Hour!

BeyondWebinar.com